Certain Unrecognized Truths:

Convict & Gang-life Discussed

by Convicts & Gangsters

an Anthology

Foreword by Tyrone Suess

Table of Contents:

Foreword

by Tyrone Suess

Where there's fire, there's undoubtedly smoke; and where there's success, there are undoubtedly haters. The publication of this book will be followed by those who will have a mouthful of things to comment on. First, they'll say that the writings herein are *telling* because, of course, we've shared some kind of *'secrets of the streets.'* Next, they'll probably say we were *lying*.

Let me help clear up some of this right off the top:

Telling, from a gangster's perspective (since it's the only perspective I know), would be if I affected the arrest of someone or otherwise adversely affected

someone's life by sharing unknowns about their actions.

Let me open that up for a moment. The people in

this book that we've shared things for, with, and about

have either, 1) been arrested, charged, convicted, and

sentenced for the crimes which were mentioned, thus

their offenses are public record open for inspection by all

and their crimes already well- known to law

enforcement; 2) They cannot be arrested, charged,

convicted or sentenced due to double-jeopardy rules and

state and federal statutes of limitations on any crimes not

related to any offense of murder; or 3) the person

mentioned is dead and has nothing to fear of being

arrested, charged, convicted, and sentenced for anything.

If it's not evident by simply *'googling'* some of

the names and events that are mentioned that there aren't

any *secrets of the streets,* than I don't know what else we

can say to you dumb mutha-fuckas (*if* the shoe fits, wear

it!). We've compiled these stories and reflected on the people known along the way and the things that have transpired insofar as to describe our culture. There are many subjects that haven't even been discussed; left untouched for the sake of preserving secrecy where necessary. Go clean up the rap industry if you're looking for a place full of people telling.

Anyone who says that we're lying should be heard. Listen to their version of events and determine for yourself if they're hating, or if they're the ones lying. What do I have to hide by lying? I've included some of the most humiliating things regarding myself and the Hoovers. *Certain Unrecognized Truths* is nonfiction. If I didn't want anyone knowing something, I just didn't share it. There are no lies lingering in these pages.

In response to those who might simply opt to say that I *"ain't shit"* –look: if anyone is upset about this book, it's more than likely because *they* 'ain't shit.'

It is more than likely because the truth *hurt* them and they are simply haters doing what haters do; *Hating*.

There are so many busters in the streets kicking it with known-snitches who have the audacity to still claim to be gangsters; yet, having essentially forfeited that right, they should be exiled from the streets but they continue to linger. I refuse to surround myself with fake, phony, frauds, many of whom overpopulate the 'streets.' These busters run around with guns, many of them willing to shoot, but when someone catches up to 'em for their foul deeds of the past, they'll quickly *tell* on the witness-stand in court. Those aren't the *'streets'* I know. Those aren't the 'streets' I'm *from*. Where I'm from, *men hold their own*.

This book is intended to raise awareness to convict and gang life. Many of the perspectives found herein remain those of the individual authors but are shared in the spirit of focusing on both the individuals and the life as a whole by giving new and perhaps different perspectives.

The hope is that awareness will reduce the stigmatized nature of the way gangs, and people who've been to prison, are seen in the world today.

Convicts and gang members belong to a culture that is often overlooked by social science. They have different norms than most other societies and live lives that are often short and brutal. These truths are most often unrecognized, but we've tried to deliver a unique perspective of the world as seen by convicts and gangsters, so, bon a petit.

Salute to the Truth!

by Warren Battle Moore

It's recognized that as a man, you have your own back at times when the path of life is most challenging. Keep your head up Homie. It is recognized that you stand tall and that you will always maintain your independence against influences that are self-destructive and non-productive to your culture and way of life. If you've weathered this storm of gang life, then you are a survivor deserving of a degree of respect that should not be infringed upon.

Not only were we born into environments conducive to a misguided path in order to find in ourselves that our destiny is manifest of our very sacrifices, but we have also stood as men amongst men against the odds that were created against us by all evil things.

Poverty, despair, poor educational systems, lack of employment opportunities, abusive childhoods, foreign-imported drugs and the consequent abuse and criminal charges that stem from those foreign and government imported "illegal substances," and, oh yeah, violence—violence like in Iraq and Afghanistan. Violence like the death penalty; violence like the police killing scores of unarmed citizens right here in America—the vast majority of whom are of the same racial background as most of the entire documented police database of gang members (black or brown).

At our present, we are seen as a cancer to the rest of society. However, gangs have suffered the same negative aspects that their 'greater community' (i.e., the ghetto) has experienced due to underlying, political, and socio-economic factors contributing to the existence of such a place.

Gang members are just as much *victims* of things like drugs, violence, and civil disenfranchisement, as the greater community around them generally is. That's because gangs are products of ghettos. Ghettoes across the nation have given birth to social cultures that have evolved over decades. These home-grown cultures are distinctly American and can lay claim to perhaps being the first bona-fide, strictly American-made culture.

You name a culture, religion, or most things, and they are of a foreign extract where America is a melting pot of imagined culture, gangs are *strictly* American. This is why I cringe when they try to compare gangs to terrorists. We are the realist culture truly made right here in America, born in the urban habitat called the ghetto. Los Angeles, Chicago, New York, and in every city and small town, there are gangs. Some of who live or have lived misguided lives, but many who are just everyday people with jobs and families, homes, businesses, etc. There are gang member actors, singers, rappers, movie stars, military veterans, and professional athletes. What is wrong with people accepting you as a gang member and allowing us to embrace our culture the same way they want everybody else to embrace everybody else's culture? We live in America people, stand up for you rights to freely associate as protected by the U.S. Constitution.

The Truth of Gang Problems

by Sam Pull Jr.

Everyone has problems so it should come as no surprise that gangs have the many problems that they have. If you look at the Hoovers and cannot see any problems, you are either blind or stupid.

If you've always felt instinctively that there was something that was just not right but you couldn't quite pin-point it, you were probably feeling the vibes of those problems.

Selfishness, and lack of both communication and leadership are just *some* of our problems. Let's look into some of those problems that exist within our gang:

<u>SELFISHNESS:</u>

Selfishness is our biggest problem. A gang is centered on unity, camaraderie, and togetherness. It is a social body requiring structure and a certain degree of cooperation in order to function properly. Without structure, no one's on the same page. It's perfectly fine for someone to have the desire to live their life individually and to themselves, for themselves; selfishness is any person's right who chooses to exercise it.

However, if someone chooses to join a gang, it must be understood that selfishness is sacrificed at that point. It's really no different than choosing to be single or choosing to start a family. A person can remain single all their life. There's nothing written in stone which forces someone into marrying and raising children. But the moment a person commits to something, their honor is invested. It is the same when joining a gang.

When a person joins a gang, they become one with the gang and there are expectations that come along with that union. A person cannot join a gang and not sacrifice selfishness. Membership in a gang demands sacrifice and when that sacrifice is resisted, it creates a problem.

Someone who wants to retain their right to be self-centered, should be removed, or remove themself from the gang and stay out of the gang's way. This is the best thing for the individual as well as the gang. The selfish person benefits by being free of the sacrifices demanded of a gang; and, the gang benefits by having one less selfish person in the way, weakening the gang with their selfish ways.

<u>LACK OF COMMUNICATION:</u>

There's no real level of common communication to establish any kind of understanding and, as a result, problems arise and ensue. In essence, the left hand doesn't know what the right hand is doing. Homies are not sharing important information and intelligence the way they should. *'Cliques'* of homies, who seldom communicate with the rest of the their gang, cause confusion and disorganization.

When homies get into conflicts with outsiders and don't communicate that conflict with other homies outside of their *'clique'* –their *other* homies are then unknowingly at a higher risk of an attack they may have otherwise been averted by such an awareness of a conflict.

When a homie gets arrested and tells on a homie and then gets out and finds some other homies to kick it with and those other homies don't even know that he's previously told on a homie, than those homies are at a higher risk of getting told on by a snitch disguised as a "Homie."

When someone gets along with one of the homies and another homie doesn't know this and consequently fucks that person off in one way or another, that person could threaten the safety of the homie he had gotten along with because neither homie ever took the time to communicate the altercation. There's millions of examples of how a lack of communication could cause problems that wouldn't otherwise exist. Communication is a simple solution to many of our problems.

<u>LACK OF LEADERSHIP</u>:

There's no meaningful leadership amongst the homies. In short, there's *too many chiefs and not enough Indians*. Evidently, everyone feels as though they're cut to be a leader and that's to be respected, but if a homie can't manage his own personal affairs to a degree where other homies can look to him and see that he's a good leader, than those "leaders" are in the way and no one should seriously consider the guidance of someone who's outwardly frivolous in what they say or do. With that being the case, homies will remain divided and forever be vulnerable to our enemies.

As men, men respect certain qualities. Men respect honor and confidence; men respect wisdom and intelligence; men respect power and loyalty; and, perhaps most importantly, men respect other men who respect the same. Young men who seek to become respectable men, will seek out knowledge of all the above in order to become a man amongst true men.

If an older homie can't teach a younger homie anything, his age alone doesn't entitle him to lead other men. And, if a younger homie won't learn anything because he thinks he knows everything, then what shape is he in to lead?

Leaders possess qualities that bring men together and can keep them together. They don't need to be the smartest, strongest, or have the most in material possessions. All they need to do is know how to bring homies together and keep them together in cooperation with one another.

To become leaders themselves one day, homies must recognize that they have to vet themselves for that kind of responsibility. They have to gain the experience necessary to wisely lead their homeboys, so that they don't lead their homeboys into destructive nothingness.

To one day be a leader, a homie must possess the qualities of patience and self-discipline. Those who will fake like they are prepared to lead, tend not to know the first thing about patience or self-discipline. All they have on their mind is being a *"Boss."* They don't want to wait. They don't have any self-discipline and ten-times-outta-ten they'll lead their homies straight into a wreck.

A true leader would just as quickly fall in line under decent leadership to keep their machine in motion, as he would step up to the plate to lead where there was inadequate leadership. If a person cannot exercise self-discipline and fall in line under principled leadership, how can they lead others? And, if a person cannot be patient enough to wait for the appropriate moment to effectively exercise their leadership abilities, than what kind of leadership skills do they *really* possess?

The worst truth of the gang life is that there are so many problems throwing us off balance yet solutions elude us as we're our own worst enemies and continue to cannibalize ourselves in layers on layers of counter-productive thought-processes that cloud our forward thinking.

With all due respect, the *clowns* who're running away with our decades-old culture, truthfully, come from a generation of *losers* who similarly experienced all of the same troubles and who also did nothing to change our course on this path of self-destruction—just like the generation before them, and the generation before them... It's generational dysfunction, but it has to end somewhere.

Why does our culture have to continuously exist for the sole purpose of destroying ourselves? Why can't we put our energies towards genuinely looking out for one another and pushing each other towards some type of successful outcomes in life? Why do we only have each other's backs when it's related to carrying out violence or rooted in getting money? If the common need for money (the motivation) were not there, would that friend still be a friend? If not, then what is the whole point of what we set out to do as comrades in this gang life? These are all questions that each gang member must seriously ask themselves if they want to preserve their culture *and* live a life that doesn't have to end so young or result in a life sentence of imprisonment.

The Controversial Truth

by Upton O'Goode

There's something going on amongst the Hoovers in Federal prisons across America. No one seems eager to discuss it, since to discuss it would be to acknowledge it as being true and to acknowledge it as being true would be to admit to a grave weakness. Thus, this truth is controversial.

No one wants to admit it, but it doesn't take away from the fact that we, as Hoovers, are weak. Indeed, we are all a reflection of one another, so when I say *we*, I mean Hoovers everywhere. If we are weak *anywhere*, we are weak *everywhere*.

The particular weakness I refer to in this instance is rooted with the Hoovers held captive in Federal prison. At the time of this writing, I was

included among the Hoovers in Federal captivity, so,
nonetheless, I speak from first-hand experience,
accompanied by utter shame in my complicit-ness.

Despite having seceded from the Crips three
decades ago, the Hoovers in the Federal prison system
still submit to Crip jurisdiction. The Hoovers in the Feds
remain under a Crip umbrella, yet, they quietly represent
themselves as *not* being Crips. This hypocrisy and two-
faced-ness demonstrates weakness on the part of The
Hoovers.

This observation will undoubtedly be viewed
un-popularly by Hoovers in the Feds, but it doesn't make
it any less true. Many Hoovers who've not visited the
Federal prison system would be surprised to realize that
the Crips dominate The Hoovers in the Feds the way that
they do.

The Crips don't seem to mind that the Hoovers have dropped the use of the name 'Crip' in identifying ourselves. Nor do they seem to mind the replacement of the name 'Crip' with 'Crim' or 'Criminal.' Indeed, it must be quite amusing to most Crips since the gesture on the part of us Hoovers is mostly hollow and meaningless under the reality of the circumstances.

Hoovers in the Feds are divided from each other in nearly every aspect. We're absorbed into the existing structure of the Crips upon arrival and have little, if any, autonomy and no independence at all. Throughout my entire term of imprisonment in the Federal prison system, we, as Hoovers, consistently adhered to the structure of the Crips. While every now and then we'd entertain the idea that we were actually an independent entity, we were always entertaining a fantasy and never acted upon it. We were weak.

I was not a part of any solution so I too was a part of the problem and was just as weak as the rest of the Hoovers. I'm not in denial like most of the homies are. In fact, many Hoover homies would rather put a knife on another Hoover to silence this Controversial Truth, than to stand up and declare their independence from the Crips and accept any consequences in doing so.

The Crips don't really seem to mind that Hoovers everywhere else outside of the Federal prison system have ceased to ride with the Crips. On the streets and in most state prison systems, the Hoovers have made a clear break with the Crips. The Crips in the Feds have surely noticed this as it is widely known and is certainly no secret. The fact that the Crips obviously know this, yet have not forced a break despite their overwhelming strength in numbers, simply goes to show that the Crips recognize the weakness of the Hoovers and are exploiting it. The Hoovers are enemies of nearly every

Crip set and, to exercise dominance over the Hoovers in one final frontier, it must be a satisfying feeling.

The Hoovers in the Feds come from various backgrounds. They come from several cities and states across the map. More often than not Hoovers in the Feds are from places outside of Los Angeles. This is in no small part due to the fact that Hoovers exist everywhere in America and that coincides with the jurisdiction of the Feds.

One of the reasons why I believe the Crips in the Feds dominate the Hoovers of the same is because the Hoovers that originate from Los Angeles tend to devote their loyalty to the Crips that originate from the same. The Hoovers who originate from Los Angeles tend to be older and/or more influential than those who are not from Los Angeles, and it is these Hoovers who have steered the Hoovers on a path following the Crips. Hoovers originating from Los Angeles tend to be more willing to devote their trust, loyalty, and confidence to Crips also from Los Angeles, forming a camaraderie which is of more or less a geographical orientation.

The Hoovers in the Feds suffer terribly from denial. Maybe not quite realizing at first how Hoovers before them have remained loyal to Crip jurisdiction despite seceding forty years earlier, by the time an unsuspecting Hoover figures out that he's under Crip dominance, he's already reliant on their establishment.

Federal prison politics consist of a complex evolution of established enemies and alliances which act and counteract with one another to balance the world that is the Federal prison system.

Although the Hoovers have declared their independence from the Crips everywhere outside of the Feds, Hoovers in Federal prison are entirely dependent upon the Crips as the Crips are an established political entity in the scheme of Federal prison politics.

In Federal prison, if you do not belong to an entity that has established themselves as such, you are hard-pressed in finding a place to sit in the chow-hall, a cell to live in, a television to watch, or a representative say in anything that goes on.

Hoovers in the Feds make all kinds of excuses to justify their surrender and continued submission to the Crips. They'll deny their weaknesses in failing to exert themselves as independent. They'll blame the Hoovers around them. They'll blame the Hoovers before them. They'll imply their lack of confidence of the Hoovers on the yard with them. They'll say that their not serving a lengthy sentence and they're going home soon. They'll quietly imply that their loyalty to the Crips is secondary to their loyalty to the Hoovers. They'll pretend that the arrangement is to their benefit and imply that they're simply using the Crips. But none of these excuses change the fact that us Hoovers are reliant on the Crips for their status as an established entity and without the Crips, we'd have to establish ourselves.

This apparent carelessness as to establishing ourselves independently of the Crips evidences our weakness. Instead, Hoovers routinely enter the Federal prison system and are manipulated by the Crips, through their own Hoover homies, to fall in line under Crip jurisdiction.

When a Hoover arrives on a yard, he' ll be approached by the Hoovers already there. They'll play on his loyalty to the Hoovers in order to persuade him to become complicit-ly loyal to the Crips. They'll move him into a *Crip* cell; sit him down at a *Crip* table in a *Crip* area of the chow-hall. They'll introduce him to *Crips* as 'the homies.'

They'll indoctrinate him to prison politics and refer to themselves alongside the Crips as 'we,' 'us,' and 'ours.' They'll introduce him to a structural hierarchy of the Crips and advise him of the chain of command which effectively eliminates any perceived independence on the part of each Hoovers hitting a yard. If a Hoover were to oppose this, he'd not be allowed to remain on the yard and, more often than not, it'll be Hoovers who force his removal.

The Hoovers quickly learn that they are second-class citizens in the Crip community. By then it's usually too late. The frustration that tends to follow only serves to breed even more discontent among the already divided Hoovers.

Each looks upon each other with disregard, almost never looking within to acknowledge their own weaknesses, and certainly never exploring any plan of action that would free them from the root of their frustration. Bickering and infighting usually ensues, leaving the Hoovers as each other's worst enemies; while the Crips bask in their victory.

The Crips tolerate the Hoovers simply because they dominate the Hoovers in a Machiavellian-manner of manipulation and control. The Crips cannot possibly have love for the Hoovers where the Hoovers have *denounced* Cripping and seceded from the Crips.

All the smiles and handshakes in the universe could not alter the truth that remains obvious to both the Crips and the Hoovers; The Hoovers obviously did not like the idea of being Crips and chose to no longer be Crips. Crips everywhere must be *disgusted* by this.

Cripping to the Crips is the center of their universe. For the Hoovers to abandon Cripping as if it were less than what the Crips believe it to be, then the Hoovers have undoubtedly offended every proud Crip in the world. Therefore, it's obvious the Hoovers can only

be viewed by the Crips with spite.

Nonetheless, in the Feds the Crips appear to

warmly welcome the Hoovers to join them and remain

with them. It's really quite ridiculous how the Crips and

the Hoovers both pretend as though everything is

completely normal. They exist together as though there's

no war between them anywhere and everywhere else.

It'd be naive to believe that the Crips in the Feds are

unaware of the Hoovers being independent of the Crips

elsewhere.

The Truth of Snitching

by Tim Purseflair

Snitching has got to be the most deplorable disease on the face of this earth. It seems to be spreading as if it were contagious. It is uncontrollable and is wiping out entire habitats, leaving many thorough species without a sustainable environment.

It's quite a shame that I'm actually going to explain some of these things, but it's obviously long overdue. Let's analyze exactly what snitching is so there are no misunderstandings. Snitching is when someone gives information to police and that information could be useful in arresting, charging and convicting someone else of a crime.

One of the most common misperceptions set forth by obvious friends and sympathizers of snitches are that if no one gets arrested, charged, or convicted of a crime, then the information given by a snitch wasn't snitching at all. Now, how fucked up is that way of thinking?

If information given by someone is even INTENDED to get someone else caught up in a criminal case, it's snitching! *Excuses* are just more encouragement for snitches to continue to tell on people. If someone tells on someone and knew, or should have known, that the information they provided to the police could get someone in trouble with the law, then they are a snitch, plain and simple.

There are no excuses and there is no coming back from snitching. You can't tell on someone and clean up your name later on and have everything go back to normal. Snitching is a permanent stain on someone's soul. A snitch is no good and will never be any good. He or she is of a nature that should forever be despised. Forgiving a snitch would encourage more snitching. In fact, the soft attitudes towards snitching these days are one of the reasons why so many people are falling victim to it.

There are three main causes of snitching. They are: 1) hatred, 2) jealousy, and, 3) fear.

1)   Hatred. When a person finds themself being hated by a snitch, they are in grave danger. A person who hates someone will tell on them in order to remove them from the picture. The snitch is usually a coward who will smile in a person's face and convince 'em that they are supportive, but they slyly hate 'em for various reasons. They might hate a person for the color of their skin. They may hate them because of the way they walk or talk. Whatever

they may hate a person for, they hate them so bad that the snitching disease just takes over and destroys. Hatred, although closely related, is different than jealousy. Jealousy arises when someone covets something that someone else has. Hatred is when a person does not covet what someone has so much as they covet them having anything at all. Hatred will fuel a person's desire of destroying someone's life, not because they are jealous of living that person's life, but because they utterly hate that person's life and everything surrounding it.

2)   Jealousy will cause someone to set out to destroy another person because they are angry that they cannot be like that other person or have what that other person has. Snitching is then a tool used to destroy someone who is hated or hated on. A person with hatred

or jealousy in their heart will often resort to snitching, especially if they are the cowardly type. They cannot gather enough courage to confront their nemesis and so when afforded an opportunity; this person will snitch with relief and a smile.

3)   Fear of prison is the probably the most common cause of snitching. Hollywood and pop culture has people pumped with fear of rapes, riots and stabbings. The statistical truth is that you're far more likely to get raped outside of prison than inside of prison. Riots are few and far in between, and, in fact, have declined in recent years with a combination of the introduction of unspoken prison politics and the weapons, tactics, incentives and punishments utilized by modern-day prison administrations. Stabbings and assaults, again, are statistically

more likely to happen to someone outside of prison than inside. Then, when someone does get badly beaten or stabbed, nine times out of ten they deserved it and had it coming for quite some time. Usually, when someone is attacked, it's only because they were a snitch, a rapist or they owed money that they could not, would not or did not pay. For a person who is in control of themselves and their actions, who does not have the type of bad drug habits that are frequently followed by bad debts; and for a person who has never been a rapist or snitched on anyone, prison has very few dangers. The smallest, frailest person could make it. That is, as long as they haven't snitched on anyone, or is not a rapist, or child molester. There are old men who walk the yard without fear of being knocked over by the younger more physically superior men. There are young men who walk the yard without

having to worry about anything at all. All of

these men have one thing in common. They are

men amongst men.

Snitching is wrong for many reasons. Snitching

is wrong because respect demands that you treat others

the way you want to be treated. No one wants to be told

on. What is worse, are the snitches who subscribe to the

lifestyle of a thorough street soldier. These supposed-to-

be gangsters, thugs, or whatever they call themselves,

are in the streets trying to make the best out of a bad

situation or whatever their case may be. They are

hustling, gangbanging, robbing, stealing or whatever,

and by living this lifestyle, they are bound to the code

which accompanies it. This code is what each person

living this lifestyle expects of everyone else living it

alongside them. The fact of the matter is that snitching is

a weakness possessed by those who would betray those

who trusted and believed in them. But snitching is not always done by people who are close. Enemies will snitch on you too. Enemies will use the police to save them when they fear they cannot win.

Police don't respect snitches either. They only respect them enough to get what information they need and they appreciate the information, but other than that, the police can't stand snitches. The police have a code of silence among their own ranks and they look upon officers who snitch on other officers as traitors. They see those officers as having betrayed their trust and confidence; just the same as almost anyone would if they enjoyed a true bond with another. So, whenever a snitch is telling on someone, the police are looking at them with very reserved opinions. In the back a police officer's mind, they're actually disgusted. They're looking at a snitch like the filthy rat they are. Thinking to themselves how glad they are that the person is not *their* friend. Even people who are not in the streets living a fast-paced lifestyle do not appreciate the betrayal of someone who they trusted.

The fact is that: snitching is not going anywhere anytime soon. It's here to stay. There always has been and always will be snitches. The best thing that each person can do is to discourage it rather than encourage it. Stop hanging out with people who are known to have snitched. Alienate them and make them feel unwelcomed. Treat them the way that you'd treat a child molester who moved in next-door. Would you let your kids play outside alone? Would you invite him over for dinner? Of course not.

Snitching has to be met with discouragement or it will become acceptable and that idea is an unacceptable one. If snitching doesn't bother you but you're living a lifestyle where you could be adversely affected by someone snitching on you, you are either a fool or a confidential informant yourself. If our younger generations see the stigma surrounding snitching and see how a person is negatively looked at and referred to, it will perhaps deter future snitching. If we go soft on snitching and allow those who have snitched to come back around and be comfortable, they will not only tell again, but the next generation will see this and think that it is okay to snitch because everyone will be okay with it.

If snitches don't get fucked up whenever they come around, they should at least not be allowed to get comfortable. No one should speak to them and no one should deal with them in any shape, form, or fashion. They should be pushed away and alienated as much as possible.

There are more drastic measures that can be taken to tighten up a person's circle too. Each time you intend on discussing something that you may not wish to be overheard, you may want to think about taking off your shirt, shaking it out and suggesting that anyone else who is there do the same. It might sound intrusive or ridiculous at first, but think about it like this: It might save you from thousands of strip searches you'd otherwise be subjected to in jail after getting told on or someone wearing a wire. What's the worse of the two evils? And, believe me; they are out there wearing wires. The shit doesn't just happen on TV.

Another way to' tighten up your circle is to conduct background checks on those who you intend to regularly hang with. You want to know what kind of homies you surround yourself with. You might find yourself in a situation where you couldn't prevent it and inadvertently end the life of another. The situation may not have allowed you to be able to pick and choose who was present when it happened.

This can be done in several ways. First, you can accompany a homie to the records division of a city's police headquarters and request police records such as arrest records and police reports. In the right hands of someone with a good attention to detail, these documents can help determine whether a person has a prior history of snitching. Background checks can also be conducted online or by hiring a private investigator to check someone out. A police printout will have police report numbers for any incidents a person has been involved in. From there, each and any police report: can be requested, obtained and examined as a matter of public record to see if a person has had a past history of snitching on someone.

In prison, most "cars" check paperwork of their homeboys to assure that they haven't snitched on anyone and to make sure that they aren't a rapist. If this were done on a more routine basis in the streets, there would be fewer snitches around telling on people.

Homies need to wise up. The streets are constantly evolving. Homies need to tighten up if they want to survive. A real homie would not be offended by other homies checking him out to make sure he's thorough. He should be glad that he has some homies who are concerned about shit like that. He should only wonder about the homies who are not concerned and why they aren't concerned.

When it is known that someone is a snitch, it should become a priority to obtain the proof to show everyone. It should be shown to anyone and everyone so that there is no question as to the certainty of the snitching that took place. The paperwork should then be kept with someone somewhere where it can be viewed at any time in the future. Homies should have a mental list of snitches that they can reference when they need to.

It should also be taken seriously if someone falsely accuses a homie of snitching. That way, it will be discouraged from homies spreading false rumors on someone. If a homie cannot prove that a homie told on someone, they should conduct an investigation to uncover the proof first, before spreading a rumor. If it is being said that a homie told on someone, it should be every homies responsibility to look into the rumor until it is certain that he did or didn't tell. The proof is not as hard to come by as some may think. There are law libraries, online databases, police records, court records, and Freedom of Information laws that can all be used to find out if someone is telling or has told. If a person is suspected of telling in an open investigation, counter-surveillance can be conducted to try to figure out the truth.

Every homie should always watch every other homie anyway. If a homie is not a snitch or is not telling, they should have no reason to protest or be angry with questions and concerns intended to keep the homies tight.

It should be considered a blessing to have homies who are constantly vigilant about whether or not someone amongst us is telling or not. We could all do better to keep our eyes open and watch each other from each other. It is only like this that we will be able to weed out the phony homies and snitches and by doing so we will become stronger. Who can be mad at that?

You don't have to kill the snitches to suppress snitching (unless you truly want to and then, by all means, I won't stop you). You can never truly kill snitching and even if you kill every known snitch on the planet, there are still snitches in waiting, just lurking in the shadows, disguised as your friend maybe, disguised as an enemy maybe, but there nonetheless. They will come out and tell on you for murdering all of the snitches probably. But, there's another way to battle snitching.

First, everyone must do their own part. You can never expect anyone to do things the same as you would as a condition of doing what you know in your heart to be the right thing. Two wrongs don't make it right. If someone tells on you, it doesn't give you an excuse to lower yourself into becoming a snitch. If someone molested your kids, you're not going to molest their kids to repay them. You are going to handle your business, but you're going to do it the way you know is *right*. The same principles apply if someone snitches on you. If you tell on them or tell on someone else, then you're no better than the person who told on you.

The police threaten to give you a hundred life sentences. They tell you that all you have to do is tell them who killed the hundred snitches. Just go to prison.

If you know in your heart that you would tell to get out, then you should acknowledge this and fall back. You should recognize this and get out of the way. If you cannot picture the possibility of yourself going to prison

for the rest of your life, you should not be in a gang. If

you cannot picture the possibility of your mother crying

over your casket at your funeral, you are in the wrong

shoes. These are all things that you must have a mental

preparation for in this life. If not, you are simply faking

and you are in the way. An in-the-closet snitch is worse

than an in-the - closet fag. A fag won't get anyone locked

up for the rest of their life, but a snitch will.

Homies need to stop cherishing the shit they

can't take to the grave with them. At the end of a life that

is all too short as it is, a homie only has his memory. The

way he will be remembered is what should be cherished.

This is true honor. How will you be remembered? Will

you be remembered as a snitch that dishonored himself

in life? A coward who was faking every minute he was

around? Or, will you be remembered as a man who

stood tall amongst men and made sacrifices whenever

you encountered adversity? Will you be remembered as a man who was stronger than the temptation that has conquered many weaker men? Will your homeboys remember you with pride? Will younger generations look up to being like you? Will the older homies wish they had more lil' homies like you?

At the end of life, the only thing that lives on is your memory. What will you be remembered for?

The Truth of the Streets

by Seymour Cash

The truth is that the Streets are an urban *habitat*. Like any habitat, the Streets are inhabited by certain species that are dependent upon that habitat's particular surroundings for their survival.

There are many species in the Streets, such as gangsters, hustlers, pimps, prostitutes (and their clientele), robbers, thieves, dope-dealers, gamblers, addicts, police (and their informants), suckers and others. The habitat of the Streets varies from place to place, but much like other habitats such as deserts, forests, or swamps, most Street habitats share many of the same characteristics with each other as they may compare to the same at a distance.

Also, just the same, whenever a habitat is destroyed or altered, certain species may thrive while others may become endangered or even extinct. There must be diversity for most habitats to survive, and a habitat deprived of certain factors can spiral a habitat into a collapse of the entire ecological structure it consists of.

The species that inhabit the habitat of the Streets also have subspecies within. In each of these species and subspecies there are behaviors and actions that are unique, often displaying some very peculiar behavioral patterns.

The Streets are full of predators and prey. The most common source of sustenance more than likely be monies; but sometimes it might be a high or another sort of fulfillment.

The Gangster species of the habitat of the Streets are powerful predators. There are several subspecies of Gangsters, and, although there are a few exceptions, most Gangsters are members of Gangs. Different Gangs are usually reflections of their surroundings, each Gang becoming unique to their environment through the evolutionary process. Gangsters belonging to Gangs adhere to principles and patterned structures of the Gang they belong to. Gangs and Gangsters are constantly evolving to adapt to their constantly changing habitats. Many Gangs and Gangsters have become endangered and even extinct due to the gentrification of their habitats. Meanwhile, the environmentalists who have moved into the areas once hosting those wild habitats, who advocate for saving other non-human species, some of which kill murder and maim other members of their own species as well as others, think nothing of the destruction of the habitat they tamed to take as their own.

With the habitat of the Streets being encroached upon more and more, the Streets are being destroyed and the native species are being displaced, captured and killed off. The habitats are being transformed into environments that are inhospitable to the species that once lived there. If a swamp is drained, the lack of water which sustains the life of much of the swamp, causes a chain-reaction that subsequently deprives, or at least effects, every species in the habitat. Many of the species of wildlife that call the swamp home depend on fish; no water would equate to no fish. Other wildlife predators that may rely on prey that in turn relies upon fish, would then find themselves deprived of their source of sustenance. This effect would reach to the top of the food chain and eventually have a devastating outcome on the entire habitat.

One of the primary threats to the habitats of the Streets is the change in climates. Not necessarily weather-related climate changes; but rather, political,

social and economic changes of climate. These changes

have caused an increase in the population of those

species which thrive in such conditions and they have

contributed to the decrease in the population of those

species which cannot survive such harsh climates (i.e., a

post-gentrified neighborhood). One of the species that

are increasing in number due to the favorable conditions

for its survival is the Snitch species. The Snitch survives

well under the encroachment of its habitat because the

Snitch is a parasitic scavenger. One of the species which

has become endangered due to the encroachment of its

habitat is the Gangster. The gangster finds it

increasingly difficult to find prey in the Streets. The

gangster has also suffered from being hunted by both

police and other gangsters. Many of the remaining

population of gangsters live in captivity.

Many subspecies of gangsters are evolving to the new habitat that they live in. In true form to the theory of evolution, only the fit will survive.

The Truth of How Black Gangs are Seen by Law Enforcement

by Tim Purseflair

In a publication titled, *The Citizens' Handbook of California Street Gangs: 1992*, which is known to have been used by the FBI in their investigation of activities of the Crips and Bloods as *"drug gangs,"* the author Paula McKibbin, J.D., points out that:

> Black street gangs are not as culturally oriented as traditional Hispanic street gangs, and they have fewer subsets. They usually only have a few older gang members. They are not as oriented or as loyal to the gang as are the Hispanics. Unlike Hispanic gang members, Black gang members put their own interests before the

rest of the gang. If a black gang member holds any loyalty, it is usually to another gang member, rather than to the gang itself. Another difference between the blacks and the Hispanics is that many black youth, unlike the Hispanics, have been known to speak openly with law enforcement officers about themselves and their gangs when they are away from their street gang comrades.

For such a publication to be relied upon by the FBI for use in carrying out criminal investigations, any crimes of which would certainly be expected to face subsequent judicial scrutiny and constitutional burdens-of-proof at a later date, the information must have been highly valued by the nation's top law enforcement agency.

The fact that the FBI actually relied on this isn't as disturbing as the fact that it's true. The reality is that,

members of black gangs have fewer older members

because black gangs, and especially their leadership, are

the primary targets of police in America. But also,

without experience or intelligent senior leadership, black

street gangs persist in knowing no better to do any better.

Its another way in which the government keeps

oppressing the mostly minority populations that gangs

are mostly comprised of.

The Truth of the Value of Worth

by Aaron Munoz

The value of worth is an interesting concept worth taking a closer look at. We as human beings have an almost natural inclination to destroy what is deemed worthless to us, whereas, to the contrary, we have an inclination to build and preserve where worthiness is appraised since it is then considered valuable. Appraisal there then is the vehicle used to close the distance in understanding why and how anything is of value to us. When we assess the value a place, it is often because of its location in relation to certain other desirable amenities. The further a particular location is from these desirable places, the less the worth. Similarly, the closer a particular location is in relation to an undesirable location, the less the worth.

Conversely, when a particular place is near a desirable location, the more it is assessed as being worth. Similarly to this example, the further distant any particular location is away from undesirable places, the more it is deemed to be worth. Market demand is often an indicator of the value of such worth.

In our personal lives, the way that we value ourselves will lead us to make decisions in our lives that are either destructive, or constructive. If we value our lives, we will work to preserve them. If we don't value our lives, we are prone to make self-destructive decisions. We assess our lives similarly to the way in which we assess the value of any place outside of our own physical and conscious selves.

We value ourselves in terms of proximity to other things that we value. If we value cars, clothes, jewelry, and things of this nature, then we will deem our own self-worth in relation to these things, and our value of worth is measured on a scale of how close we are to attaining or having, or how much has been had or attained of these things and we have suddenly appraised ourselves accordingly.

The trouble is that, things of material are simply not the most valuable things in life. The more valuable things in life are things we can still possess even when life itself expires. Our memories, our reputations, and our families who survive us, are all things of higher value than the material things that are passed along when life ends. We should look at our lives and re-assess the value of our own worth.

How distant are we from those things of highest value? How close are we in terms of achieving a high worth for the things we value? How will we be remembered by those who we love? How will be seen by others we respect? Is your life worthless and scheduled for demolition? Or, upon closer examination and assessment, is your life worth enough to preserve and build around it? It all begins with value. Next, location, location, location; you need to place yourself as close as you can to those things that are most highly valued in *your* life. That's the truth.

The Truth about Hoover Street

by Tyrone Suess

Ever wonder where Hoover Street got its name? Many people mistakenly believe it was named for Herbert Hoover, the 33rd U.S. President, who is largely blamed for the Great Depression of the 1930's. Some believe that since Hoover Street is located in a section of Los Angeles that is known for its abject poverty that perhaps the street running through this area was named for the depression-era President, but this isn't true.

I've also seen commentary where it was suggested that the street was named after J. Edgar Hoover, a closeted homosexual and former Director of the FBI. This suggestion is ridiculous since those who have always lived in the area will tell you that it was named Hoover Street before J. Edgar Hoover was ever even considered for the job that would bring him into the type of spotlight that could possibly earn himself a street named after him.

So, if Hoover Street isn't named after President Hoover or the former-Director Hoover, then who was it named for?

Hoover Street is named for Dr. Leonce Hoover, born Leonce *Huber* in Switzerland and studying medicine at the University of Paris, he'd serve in the French army as a military surgeon under Napoleon Bonaparte before eventually migrating to America to settle with his wife and three children in Los Angeles, California in 1849. Upon doing so, Dr. Huber soon changed his last name to Hoover.

Dr. Hoover was a vintner who grew what was known at the time as being some of the highest quality grapes in the region and helped pioneer Southern

California wine-making. His eldest of three children,
Vincent A. Hoover, his only son, became a Los Angeles
land developer and an early politician elected to the Los
Angeles City Common Council during the Civil War,
when California was a Union state far from the actual
conflict in the East.

In 1874, Vincent Hoover was one of the first
founders of Los Angeles County Bank which had just
taken over what had been the *Farmers and Merchants
Bank of Los Angeles*. Vincent died in 1883, but in a
development project that stretched beyond his death, the
first residential subdivision within the boundaries of
University Park was recorded in May 1875 by Vincent A.
Hoover.

The Hoover Tract, originally extending from
Adams Boulevard on the south to 23rd Street on the
north along the west side of Toberman Street, proved to
be an optimistic gesture, for serious suburban settlement

within the district did not get underway until 1887, and lots in the Hoover Tract went largely unsold.

Nevertheless, in 1892, one of the first main thoroughfares to be carved through the *Hoover Tract* was Hoover Street. At the time, L.A.'s population was about 50,000. It would eventually grow to include the further connecting thoroughfare to follow, which carried the Street well south several miles. As urban progression caught up with Hoover Street, it would encompass several miles in length running north-to-south through what is now South [Central] Los Angeles.

The Truth about the Hoover Groovers Becoming Hoover Crips

by Upton O'Goode

There has been much speculation as to when, where and why the Hoover Crips evolved into Hoover Criminals, but through much of this conversation many remain unaware that the Hoovers, as a gang, existed even before the Crips themselves did. The Crips, or Cribs depending on who you ask, were founded circa 1969-1970, however, the Hoover Groovers were a West Side gang before then; believed by many to have been around for the better part of a decade by the time the Crips were founded. With only bits and pieces of oral history surviving the harsh environs of the South Central Los Angeles gang-scape over the past half-century, much of what is left for examination remains under speculation.

Stanley "Tookie" Williams, a co-founder of the Crips who was executed in 2005 by the State of California, in his 2004 memoir, Blue Rage Black Redemption, shared an account that is as interesting in part as it is questionable. He said:

There was a problem brewing with another west side gang, the Hoover Groovers, who dressed exactly like the West Side Crips. Things had gotten out of hand when Little Chocolate, a member of the Hoover Groovers, was murdered. The mysterious killing of Chocolate and the shootings of other Hoover Groovers were blamed on the West Side Crips, but mainly on one person, Buddha. West Side Crips were ambushing the Hoover Groovers regularly, but neither

Buddha nor any West Side Crips killed

Chocolate. Buddha did hate him. While in

Factor Brookins, Buddha had held a lit

cigarette to Chocolate's forehead and dared

him to move for such a long time that I had

to snatch his hand away. Chocolate was not

an innocent bystander. He couldn't fight a

lick but he fancied himself as a pistoleer and

was a known shooter for the Hoover

Groovers. Through Bimbo, I befriended

some of the leaders of the Hoover Groovers

when I attended Brett Harte Junior High.

My homeboy Fat Riley came bearing an

olive branch from the Hoover Groovers for

a sit-down at Saint Andrews Park on

Manchester Boulevard, a park we had

anointed as our own. When Boo, Diamond,

Donnie Boy, and Big Chocolate of the

Hoover Groovers showed up, they were surprised to see the large throng of Crips and Criplettes hanging out, some playing football. They had to walk past them to get to where Buddha and I were sitting on a park bench. Bonnie and a few Criplettes were watching, sitting in the children's swing set. It was probably by design that Big Chocolate spoke for the group. Although he and I had known one another since Brett Harte, things were different now that his younger brother had been killed. He started off with, "Rumor has it that Buddha killed Little Chocolate." Buddha jumped up and said, "What, fool? If I had smoked Little Chocolate, I'd tell you right here, right now. If you truly believed I was the killer, you wouldn't be here! We'd still be at war." I calmed Buddha down, then told Big Chocolate, "Buddha didn't kill Chocolate, none of us did. But time will reveal all." Big Chocolate went on to say they wanted to establish an alliance but not until they learned who was responsible for the killing. Buddha rudely interrupted, "Look here, dude. We're the Crips. We don't need anybody!" I could sense Big Chocolate was trying to be patient so I eased the tension by appeasing them both. I said, "Buddha is right, we don't need anybody, but Big Chocolate, you're right too. An alliance will benefit all of us. We can seal the alliance when we smash whoever smoked Little Chocolate!" The mention of revenge brought a smile to Big Chocolate's scarred face and to everybody present, even Buddha.

Though no master strategist, I knew that a prolonged war with the Hoover Groovers would create chaos among many of my homeboys who had relatives in the Hoover Groovers. The last thing I needed was a division within our ranks, so I was willing to forge the alliance. As soon as I shook hands with Big Chocolate and his homeboys, they left. Buddha smiled and said, "Cuz, you are a shrewd character." I shot back, "And you, my cousin, are a crazy, crazy character!" I told him I needed him to calm down because his outbursts could mess up my plans. I understood his frustration. I too was tired of all the drama but more and more I was learning about the need for tact and diplomacy. This was a street war on a smaller level; however, there was no difference between our mindset and that of a nation seeking to eliminate its enemies through whatever method...life or death! The Hoover Groovers held the Figueroa Boys responsible for smoking Little Chocolate. The Figueroa Boys were already our rivals, and attacking them fit in with my strategy. But not only were they difficult to find, they operated with the stick-and-move ambush tactics of guerrillas. The Figueroa Boys were notorious for popping up when least expected and spraying the area with bullets. Fighting hand-to-hand was an alien concept to them. A pistol or rifle was more their speed. They were quite deadly until more Crips began to arm themselves. Then things changed. Wherever the Figueroa Boys were discovered, they were ambushed

*with a hail of hot lead, something they
weren't used to. Then fate dropped our
enemy into our lap. The leader of the
Figueroa Boys, R.M., happened to be in a
nightclub on Vermont where the West Side
Crips and Hoover Groovers planned to meet
up. When we entered the club, one of the
Hoover Groovers recognized R.M. partying
on the dance floor. For him to look up and
see the room filled with enemies staring him
down was a nightmare. I'm sure he wished
he could turn back the hands of time. His
scrawny body bounced from fist to fist like a
Ping-Pong ball till he bounced into
Buddha's knuckles, which knocked him
smooth out. Even after R.M. had been Crip-
stomped twice and riddled with bullets to his
chest, the deadly sneak-up artist and*

gunslinger survived the vicious ordeal. Later,

the Figueroa Boys seemed to fade away.

Word had it that R.M. and some of his

homeboys moved to Pasadena or Pomona.

Either way, the terror of the Figueroa Boys

was a thing of the past. The alliance with the

Hoover Groovers—now known as the

Hoover Crips—had been cemented in

violence.

Tookie said that the Hoover Groovers, "dressed exactly like the West Side Crips." Quite naturally, the question itches to be asked, how that could be if the Hoover Groovers existed before the Crips?

It appears as though Tookie, in his seemingly conflicted account, respected the Hoovers and saw the strength in their joining together with the Crips, yet it also appears as though he necessitated demeaning them just enough to give a reader the impression that the Crips were somehow the tougher of the two. The fact remains, however, that, despite any Crip attitude of superiority, the Hoovers are as resilient as gangs come; not only preceding the founding of the Crips, but also by seceding from the Crips alliance despite the overwhelming odds against them, and then continuing to survive to our present-day while surrounded by mostly enemy Crip gangs that have unsuccessfully attempted for decades to extinguish the fierce existence of the Hoovers.

It should be noted that there are certain OG Hoovers who do not recognize Tookie's account and deny that the Hoovers pre-date the founding of the Crips. Those appear to be Crip-centric members who also disapprove of the evolution of Hoover Crips to Hoover Criminals, and it further appears as though their memory is guided along the lines of conservative Crip-pride, and yet, to-date, these denials have never countered Tookie's account with any factual substance in which an alternate version of this history is described.

One of the most common alternative histories you will hear is that the Hoover Groovers were a "football team." It'd lend more weight were it discussed in greater detail what type of *league* the supposed *team* existed within or what other type of organized football association existed in South Central L.A. during the 1960's and early 1970's in which a team would name itself to differentiate itself along the lines of a geographical area such as Hoover Street.

It is argued among certain OG Hoovers, and I have personally sat and listened in on such debates, that the claim that the Hoover Groovers were actually some sort of *football team* were claims made by Hoover OG's that moved into and joined the Hoover sets AFTER previously being members of gangs on the East Side of South Central Los Angeles.

On the East Side of South Central, it was thought that the gangs were more hardcore than the gangs on the West Side. The East Side was poorer and the West Side was considered a better side of South Central L.A., beautified with wide palm-tree lined streets. So, on the East Side, they tended to see West Siders as weaker than the poorer East Siders who considered themselves tougher since their neighborhoods tended to be tougher altogether. As a result, it is argued by most Original West Side OG's, of which Tookie was very much considered, that the East Siders insulted certain other gangs from the West Side by referring to them as mere *football teams*, which thereby stripped them of the recognition required to be considered a real gang.

If OG Hoovers are still arguing about this subject to this very day, then the divisive intent of the claim made by former East Side gang members worked.

Me, myself, I'll take Tookie's word for it and he wasn't

even a Hoover.

The Truth about the 107 Hoovers

by Tyrone Suess

When passing along versions of oral history, it must be understood that there are many accounts that differ. The following is one version of the story behind the founding of the 107 Hoovers. Perhaps its safe enough to warrant saying that sharing this version of the truth may rely on the amount of faith you credit it as being true.

In a *Kev Mac* -produced documentary interview, OG Hawkeye, founder of the 107 Blocc Crips, recalls the founding of the 107 Hoovers by Frank Jones, a/k/a "Mook" in 1975.

Hawkeye says that he was in an alley spraying 107 Blocc Crip on the wall when "Mook" said, "Cuzz let me see that spray-paint can."

OG Hawkeye reminisced:

I'm thinking he gon' write Nine Deuce

Hoova, cause he was really UG (Under

Ground Crip) but he had turnt Nine-Deuce

wit' Bloodstone and them. I give him the

spray-paint can—'shit nigga; one-owe-

seven Hoova nigga'—he was like, 'damn

Hawk, nigga that'd be hard Cuzz!' I was

like, 'Mook, 107 & Hoova in Denver Lane

hood!'

(Mook said) 'I don't give a fuck Cuzz! We

gon' take that shit from them niggas!'

That was his thinking. Shit, I looked up and

Mook-Mook done started recruiting. And

then the original UG, Ronald/Country, and

all them, they was like, Yay-Yay and Leroy

and all of 'em was like, 'Ay Homie, shit, you

*ain't gon' start no 107 Hoova right here.
This Under Ground 'hood.'*

*Mook was like, 'Cuzz, I can start whatever
set I wanna start Cuzz, you know what I
mean? We all Crips and shit.'*

*They was like, 'Hoova is waaay over there,
how you gon' start some Hoovas over here
and Hoova way over there?!'*

*So they argued about it. That was the first
time I ever seen, uh, my homies, I was in the
party, my first time ever seeing in my life,
homies that was Crips shoot at another Crip.*

*Mook said, 'Cuzz, they said I can't start no
107 Hoova over here Cuzz. I can do what I
wanna do.'*

*We had a meeting over the shit at Sportsman
Park, and Raymond Washington came, and*

*we all went to 113th, Melvin Hardy, Tookie,
all of us, like, they like, 'Cuzz, they can start
a Crip set wherever they wanna start a Crip
set.'*

*Ya know Mook, like, he vowed, "Cuzz, I'ma
take that from the Denver Lanes," 'cause
they was like, 'how you gon' start some 107
Hoova and that's Denver Lane 'hood?' He
(Mook) vowed that they was finna take that
over from them. And then, um, shit, I went to
the pen, come back two years later, and, um,
I bailed down there and about a hundred
Hoovas down there.*

*I give up the Crip call, Cuzz, nobody giving
it back up to me. I'm like, 'god damn, shit,
we all give up the Crip whistle—give up the
Crip sign.' Ain't nobody giving it up to me*

so I'm like, I get all the way close and I say,

'Ay Mook!'

Mook steps forward and I ask, 'Mook, why

everybody acting all strange and funny?'

Mook said, 'Cuzz, you ain't knowing?!?'

'We get into it wit' everybody across

Normandy.'

Mook said, 'Hawk, you been in jail nigga

and when you go to yo' 'hood homie, they

gon' let you know what's been going on.' He

added, 'don't walk over here no mo' like

you used to.'

The past and present truth is that, since the
founding of the 107 Hoovers in 1975, the intersection
and adjacent area of 107th Avenue (700 block west) and
Hoover Street (10700 block south)in South [Central] Los
Angeles has remained occupied by the Denver Lane

Bloods. The 107 Hoovers' actual turf is centered in the

low-100-avenues, more on Budlong Street than not.

The Truth about the Hoover Crips Becoming Hoover Criminals

By Upton O'Goode

The following is a first-hand account shared by Tran Monroe, 50, better known as Big ZHane from L.A.'s 59 Hoover Criminals. He's currently serving a life term of imprisonment and is housed at the Federal Correctional Complex in Victorville, California.

So, let me apologize for all of the Homies that were not in the proper position to abreast y'all on the transformation that took place in the L.A. County Jail back in 1989! There might have been forty Grooves in the Gang Module 2100-2300, being that they closed the original Crip Module 4800 in late 1988. Anyway, we have a Homie named Big Hawk from Nine-Foe who loved the song Criminal Minded by KRS-1 and would always be rappin' it as he would walk the tiers sweepin' and shit. Now Lil' Scoobie from Seven Foe hit the module in like summer of 1989 and because of some of his past deeds, we had a riot with the East Coasts. After that major clash with the East Coasts, we had went on full set trip mode! Some of the East Coasts ran on the tier with the 8-Trey Gangstas and locked the gate so the Homies couldn't get at them. The Gangstas that were present on the tier didn't feel that our beef had anything to do with them (not including Big Mad Bone from 8-Trey Gangstas—he went harder than a lot of the Grooves that was there). After that, Big Hawk got into it with the Grapes about the television and went on their miscellaneous Crip tier by himself, yellin' "I get a good feeling when I go Crip killing!" Of course they all felt disrespected, but didn't want the problems that would have come with expressing what they felt. Along the way, there were a lot of different small issues with Crips that were there with us and a handful of in-house issues that lead to the meeting that took place on Baker Row amongst the Grooves; where the vote went down to change the 'C' to represent Criminals rather than Crip. A lot of the Grooves wasn't feeling it but it was enough of us on Baker Row that *was* with it so it just stuck. Some Homies came through the County during that time on their way to the Pen, or Y.A. that didn't understand and went on their journey telling the Homies that we were down in the County tripping; but they were just mistaking certain Homies getting

disciplined as punishment for not being with

the transformation—which was the farthest

thing from the truth. Anyway, I was the first

Hoova Criminal to hit Pelican Bay in

December 1989, and was the youngest

Groove there (20) at the time. The big

Homie Hoova Rob from Nine-Deuce

expressed his disapproval about the

Criminals and all that, but I stood my

ground and let him know what it was and let

him know that he had a right to feel how he

felt but, "with me, its Hoova Criminals!"

Hoova Rob said he'd just holla at Big Hawk

when he got there from the County.

However, there were Homies coming on

each bus from the County Jail who were

pushin' Criminals and wasn't nobody tryna

holla! In fact, most of the big Homies who were there understood our position and respected it, and we all coexisted. When Big Hawk finally caught up with Hoova Rob at Pelican Bay, he ultimately started pushin' Criminals as well! Now as far as it going to the streets, of course some of the Homies that were in the County with us when the transformation occurred went home, and I can only assume that that's how it spread in the sets. I had to fact-check Big Vamp (92) when we ran into each other at USP Lompoc in the early 2000's because he came out of ADX speakin' like he was Mr. Criminal, when he only heard of *us*. I let him know I was there and my hand went up and was counted in the voting, "so stop it!" So, that was all it was to it when it came to the transformation from the original 'C' versus

the summer of 1989 'C'! H's!

The Truth about Aiding and Assisting Homies

by Warren Battle Moore

Once upon a time, in a war that history knows not—as history is recorded by those who would just as soon appreciate the destruction of our kind—I was a soldier in a war that remains forgotten to the world existing outside of the one from which I came.

As a soldier in this urban war fought most of my life, I found in my personal experiences that fellow soldiers would not hesitate to give me armaments and ammunition when needed, however, when the need came around to anything else in life unrelated to the battlefield, for the most part, I was regularly and ordinarily alone in securing the assurance of my own survival.

Resources, transportation, knowledge, and wealth were not as readily shared, but nonetheless, I obtained them. In fact, in my decades gang-banging, I've seen some outright selfishness that could not be explained. I've seen Homies homeless and hungry, who weren't on drugs, and who had never otherwise dishonored themselves or their gang, be ignored by so-called Homies who were in positions to help, but plainly put, *wouldn't*. I've seen Homies holler how they'll *ride-and-die* for the Homies, but don't even take care of their kids.

The battlefield, however, is not the only place a war is fought. It's demoralizing to see this. Aiding & assisting means more than just aiding and assisting in *battle*; it means that we are all for one and one for all. It means that we must aid & assist when and where we can, when it doesn't mean removing from what a Homie needs for themselves, and sometimes, a real good Homie, does more than he can. Those are the good ones.

For the most part it seems that Homies are truly quicker to come off the hip with a weapon for a Homie than they are likely to pick a Homie up fresh –out of prison and drive him to the DMV to get situated with some ID; or take the Homie to the Social Security Office for a social security card; the parole office to check in with his P.O.; the bank to open a checking and savings account and obtain a secured credit card; or to coach them in the direction of the financial aid office of a local community college or trade school in order to get them enrolled in courses that will bring them a trade or skill-set that will ultimately bring them individual strength and resources, which will then, in turn, add strength to our collective energy. In this manner, we can grow to become rich and attain a greater sense of what freedom is.

The Truth about Gang Activity

By Reverend Robby Ray

I get what they mean when they refer to *gang activity*. What I don't get is why they insinuate *criminal activity* when they refer to *gang activity*; when the actions that are being referred to only comprise a small fraction of any gang's overall activities.

Most of us are from the bottom—a place for which most natives of will argue is quite different from the gentrified world we now live in. Shit is not *that* serious out here anymore. I won't lie and pretend for one moment that the world today is near at all the intensity of the nineties, or even the 80's or 70's. Shit *has* changed. Cameras are everywhere. People are recording things, including police brutality and steady slayings of young unarmed black men (who most gang members fit the description of). Everyone else is only seeing the very most negative aspects of our world's reality, but for gang members there is much more to the life as a whole.

The world is a different place and many gang members for the most part have calmed down. This is reflected in nationwide crime statistics.

Nowadays gang members can be found with steady employment, raising their children, and interacting more with greater-society. We, as gang members and down-to-earth people alike, enjoy gathering for cookouts and other types of social gatherings that doesn't always necessitate trouble for anyone.

A group of people getting along is NOT the problem in a ghetto and the truth is that many peaceful functions take place without police or media having any idea because no one gets shot most of the time. The trouble is that sometimes those tribes that band together clash with other tribes of men standing in honor and togetherness against their own adversities. The same as nations have for thousands of years.

Right or wrong, in the same manner in which nation-governments clash in war, and as often as state-sanctioned executions take place per government prerogative, how is it a *worse* wrong when smaller groups with differences of their own conduct themselves similarly? As well, government-imposed taxes, penalties, fines, and such sound eerily similar to the crimes of robbery, ransom and extortion codes defined by statutes.

Headed into the future, police are becoming more and more militant. Actually, it's nothing new to America, since the Department of Defense's 1033 Program has been arming local jurisdictions of law enforcement with military hardware since 1997, much of it brand new.

In an attempt to beef up occupation of the areas

where there are gangs, who can be blamed for whatever

crime they have in that area where, more often than to

remain innocently *coincidental*, it is usually the only

place they actually look for crime—black neighborhoods.

A government audit found that, since 2005 alone,

the federal government has shelled out a half trillion

dollars in military equipment to local city and county

law enforcement agencies in nearly every state. Facts

have it; in 2011 and 2012, the ATF found a mere total of

6,825 illegal handguns by gang members, 9 a day, in the

entire U.S., out of more than 2,000,000 gang members.

Despite the call to military arms that police have

basically sprinted forward towards, the ATF only found

8 gang members with Machine Guns in the entire U.S. in

all of 2011 and 2012! Out of what the FBI estimates to

be more than 2,000,000 gang members across the Unites

States, only one in 193 were found with guns in a two year period. This means that every 1-in-169 of the entire U.S. population, all who have rights but are held persecuted for belonging to a culture that is not the greater population's own.

Politically suppressed through social disenfranchisement laws; there were only 8 gang members with machine guns in a two year period! Look at the numbers in comparable terms. Evidence that gangs are chilling; the very fact that despite gang membership having risen exponentially in the past few decades, and further despite the fact of the losses in numbers that gangs have taken to both the cemetery and the penitentiary; yet the national crime rate is at a thirty year low according to the FBI's own Uniform Crime Report.

More gang members? *Less* Crime? Hmmm…How do these facts support our police arming themselves like a military force and keeping lists of gang members like they do with their program called

GANGNET?

This is real shit, I can't even make it up. These

militant police forces, the same of which are

assassinating mostly young blacks in the streets, the

same character description of most street gang members

who all, of course, are maintained on lists for gang

membership which amounts to their cultural identity?

Existing criminal databases, such as the FBI's

National Crime Information Computer, already hold the

type of cells found in the GANGNET programs

operation. The same characteristics present in the

categorical information collected in the NCIC database

is already capable of holding the same information

regardless of the additional collection of information

pertaining to one's culture. That person then can be

judged for their prescribed beliefs and principles which

are *supposed* to be tolerated in America by a tiny device

known better as the U.S. Constitution.

The police could all the same keep record of

what religious preference people lived by; or, people's

sexual orientations. Society is giving the police powers

that they are going to find hard to take away when the

next target becomes their own demographic or their own

cultural identity.

The Truth of How Vulnerable Gang Life is

By Aaron Munoz

As Hoovers, indeed, as gang members at all, most of us hail from ghettoes across the map.

In these ghettoes, we all know what can be found. Poverty and despair, police brutality, drug epidemics, above-average unemployment, poor education, and, of course violence as a normal means of dispute-resolution and/or accomplishing one's ends, as many of us feel excluded from the legal system where disputes are resolved in mainstream society.

For those of us who hail from the streets, we overstand that we have been excluded from society, and not the other way around. However, as we were given the hand we were dealt, we simply Grooved forward in life with our best step forward in whichever direction was available.

At most intersections of life, we found that we were excluded from the bigger picture society had painted mostly-only for themselves. And so, the ghettos, or the streets, as they are often referred to as, are the birthplace of gangs.

Gang structure and the community and culture that developed and evolved from that birth was also influenced by the harsh realities of the habitat from which we grew. In a sense, gangs were created by the ghetto, and not the other way around as mainstream society might have the world believe. The ghetto that manifested what we are was a result of failed government-imposed social and economic policies, and not the other way around.

In a study conducted by scientists at Queen Mary University in London, their research indicated that as much as 86% of gang members suffer from Anti-Social Personality Disorder.

With such a great percentage of gang members suspected as having Anti-Personality Disorder, perhaps we should take a closer look at what it is.

To be clear, the context in which the term anti-social is applied to the term, does not mean a person is opposed to socializing; but, instead means that a person diagnosed with Anti-social Personality Disorder is opposed to society, their rules, norms, laws, and acceptable behaviors.

Here is how the American Psychiatric Association describes it:

Antisocial Personality Disorder is a diagnosis assigned to individuals who habitually and pervasively disregard or violate the rights and considerations of others without remorse. People with Antisocial Personality Disorder may be habitual criminals, or engage in behavior which would be grounds for criminal arrest and prosecution, or they may engage in behaviors which skirt the edges of the law, or manipulate and hurt others in non-criminal ways which are widely regarded as unethical, immoral, irresponsible, or in violation of social norms and expectations. Those with APD often possess an impaired moral conscience and make decisions driven purely by their own desires without considering the needs or negative effects of their actions on others. Impulsive and criminal behavior is common. The terms psychopathy or sociopathy are also used, in some contexts synonymously, in others, sociopath is differentiated from a psychopath, in that a sociopathy is rooted in environmental causes, while psychopathy is genetically based.

The DSM-5 goes on to say that:

Individuals with Antisocial Personality Disorder tend to be charismatic, attractive, and very good at obtaining sympathy from others; for example, describing themselves as the victim of injustice. Some studies suggest that the average intelligence of antisocials is higher than the norm. Antisocials possess a superficial charm, they can be thoughtful and cunning, and have an intuitive ability to rapidly observe and analyze others, determine their needs and preferences, and present it in a manner to facilitate manipulation and exploitation.

Anti-Social Personality Disorder is a serious mental illness. The American Psychiatric Association's Diagnostic and Statistical Manual does not specify any type of treatment for Anti-Social Personality Disorder and also states that, "There are indicators that Antisocial Personality Disorder is a result of a genetic predisposition in that the individual is born without conscience."

The DSM-5 also discusses how attempts at punishment fail those with Anti-Social Personality Disorder:

> Incarceration may not be an effective deterrent to the antisocial individual, as those with APD have difficulty learning from mistakes, are rigid

in decision making, and are typically unresponsive to punishment. A primary reason that individuals with APD are often non responsive to punishment and deterrence is an inner belief system that views constraints and consequences as a rudimentary function of society, a group which they do not see themselves a part of. The antisocial may see themselves as existing above or beyond society, and thus their existence need not be confined to society's limitations and restraints; and on the contrary, those limitations and restraints are best utilized when exploited to the full advantage of the individual. As a result, for many with APD, incarceration may only serve to reinforce their primary belief system and have little effect towards future deterrence.

The DSM-5 goes on further, explaining that:

Antisocial Personality Disorder will typically have strong impacts on most areas of functioning. Persons with APD may face incarceration as a result of their criminal actions, premature death from violence or accidents, or loss of assets or property from reckless spending or civil forfeiture of assets. Divorce, separation, unemployment, financial dependency on state relief sources, homelessness, anxiety, depression, and suicide rates are all elevated in individuals with Antisocial Personality Disorder when compared to the general population. Antisocials also have the potential to cause great harm to those around

them, including family, associates,

neighbors, and complete strangers, through

financial exploitation, theft, emotional abuse,

assault, sexual assault, and homicide.

Also noted in the research conducted at Queen

Mary University, published in the Journal Personality

and Individual Differences, researchers believe joining a

gang may be the only way antisocial individuals can

make friends, fit in, and feel as if they belong (an innate

characteristic that even an antisocial individual needs).

So, in essence, it is suggested that gang

members have actually formed their own society. With

that idea in mind, is it not possible then for there to be

those outside of us, who meet all of the same criteria

described in the DSM-5, who are Anti-(against) our

society?? If our gang is our society, and they are anti-

gang, as most of mainstream society deem themselves;

then it would stand the same to say they are anti-social

towards our society, would it not??

Nonetheless, whether we are all mentally

disabled as they say we are or not, the fact of the matter

remains that the habitat from which we came certainly is

such a harsh place that most of us gang members have

for the most part been vulnerable to every type of

adversity imaginable.

The trouble is that we are not provided the care,

support, or treatment needed to overcome these

adversities unless we disown that from which we came.

Their hatred and intolerance of our kind is so great that

they require us to be an *ex*-gang member or a *former*

gang member in order to be accepted. And even then, a

former gang member can still never be wholly included

into *their* culture. However, at that time, you have

betrayed your gang's culture, history, and society, and

traded it all in in order to become a puppet in their anti-gang (anti-social) approach to solving problems that existed even before the gangs did. The Homie who does so, submits to the *problem-causers*, and solves nothing.

If Homies truly wish to solve the many problems that plague us individually, and as a whole, then we need to stand together and stop walking away to 'solve' them, and instead sit down with the Homies and figure out a better way ourselves!

The good news out of all this is, Anti-Social Personality Disorder can qualify you to receive Social Security Disability benefits from the Social Security Administration. So, since you are mentally disabled, you certainly ought to apply for this benefit that is available to you. You might be 'manipulating the system,' but, then again, that's one of your symptoms when you have Anti-social Personality Disorder, so go get the benefits you're entitled to!

The Truth about Associational Inequality

by Warren Battle Moore

If the way in which we see our gang takes a place in our lives that a religion would take in another individual's life, would it not be safe to presume that our gang is our religion? It is certainly held so in the Federal courts that if a belief system takes the place that god would ordinarily fill in a monotheistic religion, then that belief system is held to be a bona fide religion. In that perspective, would it then also not be offensive every time we heard the term "gang-related" to refer to a crime committed by an individual and not the gang as a whole? When a Jew is arrested for drunk driving, they will not say the underlying offense of the individual is "Judaism-related." Nor do they attach the term "Catholic-related" every time a Catholic is arrested for molesting a child; or,

"Muslim-related" to describe a terrorist act. Why then do they prescribe the use of the term "gang-related" to every crime committed to by every gang member? The answer is simple: We let them.

If the police announced that a man was arrested for touching a little boy's pee-pee, and that they believe the crime was "Catholic-related," there would be extreme backlash. The pope would denounce the U.S.; they'd certainly sue whatever newspaper, and their source. But what do we do when they describe a crime as "gang-related?" Short answer: Nothing. Need a longer answer than that? Absolutely nothing. Yet, most often, these crimes that are termed as "gang-related" are committed by individual gang-members; often someone we, as gang members, have never known or met, we stood to gain nothing from their actions, and was more than likely the individual interpretation of what that gang member believed was a sacrifice for himself or maybe,

just *maybe* his gang.

Why is the culture we belong to suddenly so

"criminal," in and of itself, when the crimes carried out

by individual members are seldom, if ever, beyond a

situation of personal pain or individual gain? To term it

as such implicates that everyone in that group indicated

was knowingly responsible for the crime committed.

Similarly, Islamic extremists are large in number and

many of them claim that they are engaged in a holy war

called for as per their individual interpretations of their

own religious views. In the politically correct context,

the majority refrain from placing the blame for these

radical interpretations as belonging to the whole of the

world's Muslims. By announcing every time a bomb

goes off that it was "Muslim-related," would seriously

make our gas prices higher than they already are. That's

the reason why the remaining non-extremist Muslims of the world are not referred to terrorists.

If our government wasn't reliant upon the natural resources of the area of the globe occupied by Muslims, they most certainly would apply a similar term in the manner executed with gangs and gang members. How then are we allowed to be labeled as criminal then, when only some of us interpret our sacrifices to their gang into something resulting in what may be a crime? Because we are poor and oppressed peoples who hold no natural resources or anything else to be exploited, except for the potential slave labor we may be able to provide per the 13th Amendment of the Constitution which gives the government, in 2019, the right to force labor upon those convicted of criminal offenses. It is why we are termed "criminal" street gangs. We are painted with the term in order to alienate us from those in mainstream society who, naturally, wouldn't want to be seen as associating with "criminals;" the whole idea being to isolate us from the remainder of the mainstream population so that we will be easier to be systematically processed into what amounts to modern-day slaves, without the general public having a care, concern, or objection whatsoever.

Who determines a gang's purposes? The gang itself, or, *outsiders*?

As individuals, we just might commit a crime; ignorant of a better way in which we may get to an end with no means or perhaps a lack thereof. However, I did not take a criminal angle at overcoming my personal obstacles with an act which my Homies had anything to do with, so why do they get punished for what I've done?

As a gang member, I fully accept responsibility for my own criminal conduct when and where it is committed, however, those actions of my own have no bearing on the individuals who identify with the same gang life style as I do; therefore the crimes I personally commit are therefore **not** *gang-related.*

The Truth about Gang "Enforcement"

by Handsome Ransom

July 15, 2013

Captain David Meyer

Portland Police Bureau

Tactical Operations Division

Gang Enforcement Team

449 NE Emerson Street

Portland, OR 97211

RE: Pending Gang Designation

Captain Meyer,

I'm in receipt of this Bureau's Notification of Pending Gang designation and I wish to challenge the preliminary determination of the allegations that the gang I belong to is "criminal." I do not dispute that I'm the member of a gang. However, I do dispute the allegations that the gang I'm a member of is "criminal." This Bureau has classified a group of persons, that group being the Hoovers, the group in which I'm an associate, as "criminal," without providing due process to that unincorporated association.

Pursuant to Federal Rules of Civil Procedure 17(b), "The capacity of a corporation to sue or be sued shall be determined by the law under which it was organized. In all other cases capacity to sue or be sued shall be determined by the law of the state in which the district court is held, except (1) that a partnership or other unincorporated association, which has no such capacity by the law of such state, may sue or be sued in its common name for the purpose of enforcing for or against it a substantive right existing under the Constitution or laws of the United States."

*Please be advised that, the Hoovers, being
an unincorporated association at common
law, do still retain certain rights. Those
rights include the Freedom of Association,
and other Due Process rights. The Hoovers
have not been afforded any degree of due
process prior to being labeled "criminal,"
and, as the Hoovers do not exist contrary to
any laws of the State of Oregon, or the
United States of America, and, because this
label of "criminal" adversely affects every
member of the Hoovers, I have standing to
challenge that label on behalf of the entire
unincorporated association of the Hoovers.*

*As such, I fully intend to challenge this label
of "criminal" being unfairly placed upon my
association. No such label of "criminal" has
been placed upon catholics despite the
rampant molestation which has regularly
occurred within that association of
individuals. This "criminal" classification
of the Hoovers is class and race-based and*

has absolutely no bearing on the individual character of each member, yet Portland Police practice this policy of labeling associates of the Hoovers since, 1) Most members are uneducated and do not understand the rights afforded them; 2) Most members are minorities that have always lived below the poverty line; and 3) Most members do not even know of this classification, or its consequences.

Essentially, the Portland Police are practicing a policy of wide-scale racial profiling that preys on minorities who grew up in impoverished and disadvantaged communities. This classification works to their extreme detriment and is aimed at further oppressing these peoples.

I stand firm by my association with the Hoovers, nonetheless, I contest the allegations that the association I'm affiliated with is "criminal."

Nevertheless, you have a great day.

That letter was written six years ago. At the time, I was fresh out of Federal prison and was still living with my mother. Since then, I've got my own apartment, I've graduated from college, started my own business, successfully completed a three year term of supervised release, and met a wonderful woman to call my wife. I've not been arrested, charged, or convicted of any crime(s) since my 2012 release. However, I'm still followed and pulled over on a regular basis, just so the Gang Enforcement Team can get a close-up look of me. They'll call the entire Team, and detain me incident to a mere 'traffic stop' for upwards of hours at a time; constantly failing at coercing me to allow them warrantless search of my lawfully licensed person and vehicle. I've video-recorded them; called and made complaints, and I've even tried to challenge the designation. In fact, the very letter seen above was only responded to with a phone call, as noted in an "Inter-office memorandum" by Sgt. Don Livingston.

What was NOT noted in that memorandum is that I was NEVER given a hearing after that. Instead, I was called in by my supervising officer at the United States Probation Office and told in so many words that I was to "let go of the issue." I took that to mean that I would be making trouble for myself with him, a man who had absolute control of whether or not I remained free in the community. All he'd have to do is say that I violated one condition or another, and I'd easily have found myself sitting in the county jail for months while any matter was pending, regardless of my guilt or innocence.

So I left the issue alone because it didn't matter anyway. Then, on September 11 of that same year, I look up and see my face on the news screen as the news segment said that "Portland Police" described me as a "high-profile gangster" and showed a seven year-old mugshot photo while discussing my past in irrelevance to a recent shooting for which I had nothing to do with whatsoever. I was originally designated as a gang member back in 1996 when they just began using the new court mandated guidelines to designate individuals as gang members.

In 2013, Portland Police were in my mother's fenced-in front yard, shining flashlights through the windows of her house. I went outside to ask what they were doing and they told me that they got a 'shots fired' call in the area and thought that since I lived so close to where the call was made from, that it might have been someone shooting at my mom's house because I was a gang member and lived there.

At the time, I was not designated as a gang member and I was aware of this and made mention as to the fact that I was "purged" from the gang list, as I told them to get the fuck out of my mom's front yard. Less than a few weeks later, I was appalled to receive a Pending Gang Designation Letter. Further appalling was that the Portland Police used the exact same evidence gathered in 1996 in order to support their assertion that I should be re-designated, as they had no new evidence to support their decision.

Here we are years after that cat-and-mouse designation-game and I'm still regularly harassed by the police. I've been pulled over with my kids in the car and they were even scrutinized as possible gang members. My 14-year old daughter was nearly taken in for "identification" because she was in my backseat and didn't have any identification. They told me that all they wanted to do was search the car and they'd let us go on our way. I refused, not because I had any contraband, but merely because I have a right to do so, also desiring to set an example for my children that they too have rights.

Another time, I was taking my daughter to her volunteer shift at the Oregon Humane Society on Columbia Blvd. and was being followed on the way there for at least a few miles. Presumably taking my turn into the Oregon Humane Society's parking lot as *elusive maneuvering*, and despite the fact that I put my blinker on a few hundred feet before I turned into the lot, one of the three un-marked Gang Enforcement Team vehicles that were following me activated their overhead lights and initiated a traffic stop.

I pulled into the Humane Society parking lot and my vehicle was instantly swarmed by officers of the Portland Police Bureau's Gang Enforcement Team.

There was an officer from Beaverton, and another from Milwaukee apparently riding alongside the Portland officers. I was "introduced," to these outside-police officers by my gang moniker, in front of both my daughter and son. We were then harassed for nearly two hours before they allowed me to go on my way.

When I asked why I was stopped, the police officer said, "you failed to signal your turn within 150 feet." My daughter was so humiliated by the entire episode that she chose to no longer volunteer at the Humane Society.

When the police pull me over, they taunt me; they like to joke a whole lot, and they always inconvenience me by detaining much longer than any traffic stop ever needs to take. Gangs are gangs and crime is crime. If a gang member commits a crime, than he will have those consequences to deal with the same as if he committed a crime and was not a gang member. Gangs are simply the fraternal associations of the poor.

Many of the people typically have no idea what they're talking about when referring to gangs or the members thereof. Police criteria for the designated gang member list was: "Three or more people....two or more crimes...." That could be the Catholics, Freemasons, Democrats, Republicans, the military, the Civil Rights Movement, gays, and the police themselves could certainly fit that description.

Many police get arrested for drunk driving—a deadly and sometimes fatal crime for which police regularly commit. Unbelievable!? Google *police officer* and *drunk driving* and you will find that it is quite prevalent among police officers to get drunk and get behind the wheel of a vehicle. Do the same search using the keywords *police officers* and *domestic violence*— their other common booking offense.

Does this make police officers a criminal gang? According to the definition they have set aside for gang members, they fit the exact same criteria. The bottom line here is that the police don't need any such list in order to do their jobs effectively. They should simply focus on crimes and criminals. When crime-fighters begin fighting cultures instead of crime, they detract resources from the purpose of their true duty. They have more than just a list of criminals; they have an entire database full of them (i.e., NCIC, LEDS, etc.). They are consequently diluting those systems' effectiveness with duplicitous records of what should ONLY consist wholly of criminals one way or another, no matter what their associational membership may be.

Fortunately, and much over-due; the Portland Police announced that on October 15, 2017, they will no longer designate individuals as gang members, and will purge their records of past designations as well.

It's about time they did something to recognize the fact that gang membership is *not* a crime, nor criminal. But, just *saying* is not *doing*, so I wanted to see how it effectively changed anything at all and so I wrote the Chief of the Portland Police Bureau the following letter:

October 7, 2017

Danielle Outlaw, Chief of Police

Portland Police Bureau

1111 SW 2nd Avenue

Portland, OR 97204

RE: Request for a Formal Apology for Gang Designation

Dear Chief Outlaw;

In 2013, Portland Police subjected me not to just a "gang" designation, but, to a "criminal gang" designation. Attached hereto is a copy of that report and my letter challenging that designation (PPB #13-69557). Since then, I've helped to raise my children, graduated from college, and haven't been arrested in over a decade. Upon my 2012 release from prison, I successfully completed a three-year term of community supervision, that was two years ago, without being violated at all, and I've stayed out of trouble, minding to my studies and personal interests, all of which are lawful. I've married and traveled, and met new friends. All this and I still consider myself a gang member. Not a criminal; just a gang member. Contrary to popular belief, the two are separate and individual of one another.

However, the point of this letter is not to rant; I'm writing to challenge the Portland Police Bureau to apologize for a real-life case of how your gang designation policy adversely affected me as I aimed to better myself. In a September 8, 2017 Press Release, Portland Police announced they will no longer designate individuals as gang members. The statement also said, "As times have changed, the Portland Police Bureau in partnership with community members have realized being labeled a 'gang member' can have a negative impact on the person who may be making attempts to overcome the challenges they face."

This Bureau's June 2013 criminal gang designation negatively impacted me in 2014 when Captain Mike Krantz, the then head of the PPB's "Gang Enforcement Team" (what exactly do they enforce again?), told a Multnomah County Family Court Services Custody Evaluator by the name of Judith Moyer that I was a designated gang member, which thereby directly affected the removal of my son from my custody. More specifically, I'll just quote Captain Mike Krantz from her report, which I can make available for you upon request (or you can ask him for a copy of the email he sent Judith Moyer):

"[Name Redacted] was contacted by the Gang Enforcement Team and they interviewed him. He claimed he was a lifelong 107 Hoover gang member and that would never change. He was also with Demetrius Brown who is a well-known gang member also and who was recently indicted for murder. [Name Redacted] attempted to take his criminal gang designation to hearings, however, he wrote a letter in which he said he did not oppose the gang affiliation but rather that it was a criminal gang. Needless to say the gang designation stands, and he is still a designated Hoover Criminal 107 gang member. He claims to be out of the lifestyle. Clearly, his police contacts would dispute that fact."

This report's source, Captain Krantz was very prejudicial and totally inappropriate, not only in the fact that he was not under subpoena or any other compelling obligation to share his opinion, yet, it was relied upon by a Multnomah County Family Court judge in subsequently deeming my *home as too dangerous for my son to remain in. Not that it mattered that the Portland Police have not arrested me for **anything** since 2007. Not that it mattered that his principal, school teacher, and school counselor all appeared as witnesses testifying as to how close I worked with my son in helping him be the great student that they also said he was. Not to mention Rob Richardson, community leader and activist testifying as well. He told the judge how gangs are generational and social in construct and how gang membership did not necessarily define one as a criminal. Nonetheless, the outcome was as you'd expect it. The City's law enforcement arm, not enforcing a criminal law in any way, interjected an official report which adversely affected the outcome in a custody case that had no other concerns involved that were criminal. The court relied on what they trusted as a professional opinion, that, essentially, gangs are criminal—which is simply not fact. So, I hereby request from* *this Bureau a formal apology for distorting my character by mere association and consequently adversely affecting my family by forming the basis for which my son was removed from his father's custody.*

The Portland Police Bureau recently appears to be committing itself to making steps in the right direction in focusing on crime rather than oppressing a culture for it being troubled, unpopular, and misunderstood. The September 8th announcement alluded that Portland Police "have realized..." In that realization, is the Portland Police Bureau realistically ready to reach out and right any of those wrongs?

Cordially,

[Name redacted]

Hoover Gang Member.

I never received a reply to the letter and frankly, I expect I never will. Nor was my activism recognized as any type of contribution toward the purging of that failed system of collecting individual gang members into a list. There is still a lot of work that needs to be done to bring fairness and equality to gang members in America, but it won't start without us gang members pressing forward and lighting the match to ignite the firestorm.

The truth is actually a lie in that being in a gang is not a criminal offense whatsoever. Thus the term "gang enforcement" then implies that gangs are illegal and the police are *enforcing* a criminal law, which couldn't be the furthest thing from the truth. If the police took note of how many self-professed *Christians* committed crimes, they could very well conclude that the Christians are indeed a gang and could then "enforce" them.

The real underlying truth of this matter is that the police are only doing what the gangs have always allowed them to do by not stepping up and challenging the oppression in the manner that police are aware that

other minority groups ordinarily would.

The Truth about Prison Mail Violation Policies

by Tim Purseflair

The short truth is that the Department of Corrections—though it *does* hate gay people—they hate gangs even *more* than they hate gay people. Let me share with you how they extend greater deference towards things of a gay nature than they do of a gang nature.

The Oregon Department of Corrections has regularly and routinely rejected mail along the lines of it being gang related without providing any real reasoning as to how belonging to a gang culture interferes with some false sense-of-rehabilitation that is not actually taking place inside prisons. The Department of Corrections denies us wholesale our freedom to exercise religion as well as our freedom to associate with those who we choose, both of which are supposed to be guaranteed by the U.S. Constitution.

It's well-known by mostly anyone who has served a term of imprisonment in an Oregon prison, that the mail rejections are disparately narrowed to rejection of "gang" content, whereas, communists, Islamic extremists, white-supremacists, homosexuals, and other unpopular, yet, Constitutionally-protected associations of individuals are allowed publications on a regular and routine basis. The term "gang content," or otherwise referred to as "STG" content, is routinely rejected on the grounds that its content is a threat to the safety, security, and orderly operation of their institutions. We also know and understand that the majority of those who are referred to as "gang" members or "STG" members, are overwhelmingly racial minorities. It is also well understood that, as minorities, the "system" has shown an age-old pattern of discrimination, persecution, and

oppression dating back hundreds of years.

With this knowledge and understanding, we

have collectively gathered experiences which support

such a conclusion. We know that the term "gang" is used

by law enforcement and correctional circles as *code* for

young Blacks, Latinos; even Asians, and Pacific

Islanders.

We see that White motorcycle clubs are targeted

separately from "street" gangs, and that those

investigations and prosecutions are given much greater

latitude of favor for the defendants in those cases, such

as reasonable bails and sentencing to less time in prison

as compared to similar offenses committed by "gang"

members for "gang" related crimes.

We see that in the course of those investigations

and prosecutions, great care is taken to treat those mostly

White members of motorcycle clubs with dignity and respect. We see that European organized crime members are investigated and prosecuted with their dignity and respect remaining intact. Conversely, we see that when "gangs" are the center of an investigation or prosecution, that they are dealt with indignantly and disrespectfully.

Anyone who has been considered by law enforcement as a "gang member" can attest to the destruction left behind by police exercising any search of a "gang" member's home, vehicle, or even their prison cell, as this type of oppression does not stop when a "gang" member is sent to prison.

Also, "gang" members can attest the disparate level of use of force in almost every interaction between themselves and police. We see that Communists, despite having an ideological belief that armed revolt against capitalist governments (including the U.S. government) as a goal, can still receive their periodical publication,

such as *Liberation News* and *People's World.*

Despite having a reputation of racism and

Islamic extremism, the Nation of Islam's *Final Call* is

allowed into Oregon's prisons as well. Though

homosexual intercourse is prohibited by prison rules,

even the homosexuals may receive homosexual

publications. In fact, according to OAR 291-131-

0035(1)(a)(D)(c), "Sexually explicit material does not

include material of a news or information type, for

example, publications covering the activities of gay

rights or gay religious groups."

The rules go on to state, "(d) Literary

publications shall not be excluded solely because of

homosexual themes or references, except for violations

of these rules;" and, "(e) sexually explicit material may

be admitted if it has scholarly value, or general social or

literary value."

As a least restrictive means of enforcing a ban on sex and all things of a sexual nature, which this Department subscribes to as a compelling governmental interest, to include hetero- and homosexual activities, the Department of Corrections rule allows homosexuals to still receive publications of the 'news or information type.'

This example brings me to the point that the ODOC has demonstrated an ability to tolerate certain homosexually-related material although they continue not to allow homosexually related behavior.

Why then can a "gang" member similarly be allowed to receive publications which are of the 'news and information type' without such an allowance interfering any differently than in the case of prohibited homosexual behavior? The reasons are simple. Not only are the majority of "gangs" racial minorities (yet a majority in most prison populations) but historically speaking, they are the least likely of any group to initiate legal and remedial actions against the establishment, of which law enforcement agencies and the ODOC are very much a part of.

Gang injunctions, for example, are mere default judgments ordered by judges who had not any legal representative of the gangs sued to argue on the behalf of respondent gangs. It is a basic legal principle that one must have 'standing' in order to challenge any contest in a court of law.

In civil law, if a petitioner, such as local law enforcement or prosecutors, petitions a court for remedial action, yet the person or unincorporated association of individuals (to include "gangs"), do not appear before that court in order to argue the case being made against them, then it is within the rules of the system of American jurisprudence for a judge to enter an order by default which grants the petitioner anything they sought as a remedy. In this instance of mail being rejected for "gang content" the assumption remains that an item or topic that is *solely* gang is *anything* criminal.

Seen by most outsiders as problematic, most of the staunchest opponents of gangs seem to know very little about them up close and personal. For some reason, the most relied upon asset of *experts* for interpreting to mainstream society the complexities of gang life are the police.

For the past few decades, gangs have matured a lot. We've grown in many ways and, today, you are likely to turn on your television and see celebrities doing the *Crip Walk*.

In fact, there are actors, musicians, singers, writers, professional athletes, college graduates, military veterans, and others from all walks of life that are self-professed gang members.

Being in a gang is not illegal. I repeat: Being a gang member is *not* a crime. Gangs have earned violent stereotypes by way of much misdirection. However, nowadays, you will increasingly find the norms have changed from those of 20 years ago. First, it's not as violent. Seriously; if you drive a car, you are much more likely to die in a deadly traffic crash than a gang member is likely to be killed in a place like Portland, Oregon.

If you are not a gang member, you have a better chance of getting struck by lightning than being killed by a gang member (that's counting stray bullets). Also, nowadays more gang members find legal employment and/or a *legal* 'side-hustle' to be the norm insofar as income is concerned.

20 years ago, most gang members, myself included, sold crack. Crack use has declined. No more open-air drug markets of the 1980's and 1990's. Shootings are down. Northeast Portland is gentrified.

Chicago had more gang-related murders just last year than Portland has ever had—ever.

The war was won long ago. It's pretty evident who won it. The *realer* reality is that the police and the criminal justice system have all but destroyed gangs and gangs are now the very most oppressed people in America.

Gangs seldom, if ever, fight back in the courts. Police and prison officials alike are used to the ignorant, oppressed, uneducated specimen of gang members they have encountered for decades. They're used to gang members informing on one another, infighting within their gangs, inter-gang fighting, and other nonsense that many gang members have unwittingly subscribed to in the past, by not knowing any better.

Police know that most of the time, gang members pose no danger to either police or the general public, as most gang members run from police before attacking police—basically, they'll attack other gang members far more than ordinary citizens or police.

In media reports concerning gang related incidents, you'll often hear the news-reporters end a broadcast by saying that there is thought to be no danger to the public. The facts stand that police kill gang members on a regular basis and there is seldom the scenario in which it is the other way around. Gang members routinely discard their weapons and ordinarily flee from the mere sight of the police.

Gangs are more endangered by the police than the police are endangered by gangs; just as gang members are more at danger of suffering harm inflicted by another gang member then the general public is in danger of suffering harm inflicted by a gang member.

If we knew better, we'd do better, and this is one

of the many ideological thought patterns we must target

for change. However, we cannot teach those who refuse

to learn. Also, we cannot teach to those who we cannot

communicate with due to unlawful, unwarranted

governmental intrusions and interference.

It must be remembered that being a gang

member is not a crime. Gangs are not illegal and have a

Constitutional Right to Freedom of Association,

Freedom of Expression, and if it applies to your beliefs

and practices, the Freedom of Religion.

Gangs are under fire for no other reason than the

system being unable to refer, due to political incorrect-

ness, to minorities as *criminals* the way that they openly

referred to them in the past before the Civil Rights

movements of the 1950's and 1960's.

With the changes ushered in during this historical era, police and prison officials were suddenly left with no way to identify the menace they saw in the minority groups here in America. Slavery was similarly abolished, with the 13th Amendment, yet slavery still exists under the guise of convicted prisoners.

Nowadays, any *good 'ole boy* prison guard or police officer knows how to describe the formerly oppressed groups of minorities without legally offending them or violating their civil rights. If anything, by targeting minorities under the guise of "gangs," these *good 'ole boys* understand that the primary target is further narrowed down to mostly the male gender of the minority groups, which were mostly always the target *before* the term became popularly used.

The acceptance by most gangs of a few white members which wholly constitutes a gross minority of every street gang in America, is the shining argument of police and prison guards as to the impossibility of their treatment towards "gangs" as being *racist* treatment.

The reality is that there are millions of gang members in America and around the world. Somewhere along the line, gangs began to be categorized as purely criminal associations. Although many gang members, being products of the environment they hail from, have criminal convictions, the fact of the matter is that those criminal behaviors are more often associated with the historical lack of opportunities nonexistent in those environments.

For example, a large and disparate number of criminal convictions come from poor communities, of which the primary racial makeup consists of minorities. So then, the gangs are less *criminal* in purpose than the established consensus of criminality suggests.

There is no such thing as a "criminal gang." Even to the extent that Hoovers refer to themselves as *Criminals*, the term was simply embraced by Hoovers as a term it was referred to as by society and its henchmen, also known as the police, prosecutors, and prison guards. A similar example is the way in which the racist term *nigger* was embraced by Blacks as a term of endearment (nigga) only after being referred to as by Whites with the word in a derogatory fashion.

Modern-day gangs were not formed and do not exist as associations of individuals committed to crime alone and gangs do not have some type of profit sharing scheme in which one gang member must share their fruits of crime with other gang members. If a gang member sells drugs, burglarizes a house, robs a bank or does anything else that profit from crime, they are under no obligation imposed by a gang to share those dividends.

Crime is prevalent in poor communities throughout the entire world and the people who come from these areas are overwhelmingly more likely to commit what is considered to be a crime by the establishment. However, this does not make every single person who comes from a poor community a criminal, nor does every person who comes from such a community belong to a gang. The assumption that all gang members are criminals is wrong. Yet, the statistics are distorted to make it seem as such.

The Portland Police Bureau, before abolishing their gang designation program, defined a gang as, "An ongoing organization, association or group of three or more individuals who use both of the following: a.) Use a gang name, common identifying sign or symbol, or acknowledge an identifiable leadership. b.) Have a high rate of interaction among themselves to the exclusion of other persons or gangs." Were the definition to stop there, the police might have stood correct, however, the definition goes on to state, "A gang is criminal if individuals affiliated with it have committed two or more crimes, which involve any of the following: a.) Benefit members of the group; b.) Are committed as part of an initiation process or membership ritual; c.) Are designed to announce the existence of the gang, its membership or its territorial claims; d.) Are committed in response to the race, color, religion, sexual preference, national origin or gang association of the victim; e.) Are designed to intimidate a victim in the name of the gang."

So, the criteria to be considered a " criminal gang" member is simplified into being an association of three or more people who have committed two or more crimes involving the pre-fabricated reasoning of why gangs exist. The Portland Police, as are most police departments across the country, meet the same categorical criteria, as does the Catholic Church, the

Freemasons, and most political dissidents. In fact, Martin Luther King Jr. and members of the civil rights movement would fit this narrow criteria since they were repeatedly arrested for crimes that law enforcement could easily argue that those crimes, "a.) Benefit members of that group." The Portland Police go even further by making it a point to document, not only gang members, but also gang affiliates. Portland Police describe a gang affiliate as, "Gang affiliate: A person who participates in either the criminal or non-criminal behavior of a criminal gang listed above, or who actively pursues membership in a criminal gang by performing criminal acts intended to gain the approval of the gang." This clause criminalizes all other persons who merely affiliate with someone who is documented by the Portland Police as a gang member

As a gang member is ostracized by a greater society existing around their own society (greater society consisting of mostly middle- to upper-class White people, and the gang society consisting of mostly impoverished racial minorities and their poor White friends) are further alienated from any future opportunities suddenly unavailable to them as "felons."

So it is then that the gang is perpetually oppressed into near and real desperation which results in a lifetime of low self-worth and systematic recidivism. So it is then that the gangs and gang members are stuck in somewhat of a rut that they cannot seemingly climb out of unless they surrender their gang membership, betray where they come from, and join those who call themselves "anti-Gang" activists, who are ultimately allied with the law enforcement and prison agencies of the government and seen by gangs and gang members as enemies, as it is in their agenda to destroy gangs.

The truth is that no one can help gangs or gang members to rise above the state of perpetual oppression except the gangs and gang members themselves. This stands to be the single greatest remedy to the problems associated with gangs and gang membership. Gangs and gang members must help themselves as themselves, not as turn-coats. Gangs and the members thereof must know and understand that they are their own worst enemies. Gangs must organize themselves and find reconciliation with their purpose and existence. Gangs must focus on strengthening themselves rather than solely focusing on weakening the next gang. Because, while gangs tend to weaken other gangs rather than strengthen themselves, only the establishment benefits from those weaknesses.

Gangs must evolve and see themselves for more than they've allowed themselves to be defined as by oppressive governmental agencies such as police and prison officials. How do we defend ourselves and our honor and culture from the offending of it by another gang, but conversely will meekly sit out a legal fight against an oppressor of everything we stand for now and for years bygone? How can a Hoover sacrifice a life of imprisonment for someone saying "Hoova Killa," but turn around and patiently listen to what someone with an "anti-gang" agenda has to say?

Steel sharpens steel—get sharp! Strap up with knowledge of the ideals set forth herein and fight back every time you're discriminated against. Learn and understand the Constitution and the rights afforded accordingly. Every oppressed people in this country's history have had to *fight* for those rights and they will not just be given to you.

The Truth about Out-of-Town Hoovers

by Handsome Cash

If you're wondering what exactly I mean when I use the term, *out-of-town Hoover*—I mean: a Hoover gang member—whether from Fo' Tray to Eleven-Duce—or any sets in between; a Hoover Crip *or* Hoover Criminal—who is **not** native to South Central Los Angeles.

Basically, the Hoovers from LA, when they move to a city anew, are *transplants*, while the Hoovers who join in and from other cities are *clones* of those transplants. Each generation therefrom is a then clone of a clone of a clone, etc.. With that being said, allow me to move forward with the remainder of the truth.

If you're wondering the perspective of the author, then likely you have a bias, since the truth is, and should always be, that only the truth matters, regardless of the origins of any author's geography. However, for the sake of fulfilling anyone's curiosity, I'll go ahead and add that the author is indeed an *out-of town* Hoover.

Let's make it clearly understood from the outset of this analysis that although its focus is the manner in which the caliber of *out-of-town* Hoovers is weighed by their native L.A. Hoover Homies, this truth *could* be all my own. However willing I am to risk being wrong by making this analysis, it's **not** made blindly and unknowingly. Indeed, it's based on more than a quarter-century of experiences interacting broadly with Hoovers from several cities in California, Oregon, Washington, Nevada, Arizona, Oklahoma, Tennessee, Texas, and more.

My experiences also include having been locked up in several states and the Federal prison system where there are Hoovers from all over America, where, often,

the out-of-town Hoovers outnumbered the L.A. originals.

I want to begin by saying that I believe that

several factors influence the styles and trends of the

clones of—not only my own city, Portland, Oregon—but

the clones of Hoovers originating in other cities as well.

Much like the cocaine that casually came with

L.A. transplants, (good looking out (the real) Ricky

Ross!) one factor is the character of the individual

transplants themselves (quality), as well as how *many*

(quantity) different Hoover transplants arrived in any

given city, and how long they were actually there to

properly indoctrinate any new Homies.

Another factor important in determining the

caliber of a Hoover clone is the time period in which the

Hoover transplants arrived. This is important because the

Hoovers in the 1980's were raised in a different period

of time and embraced a different set of ideals which were trimmed only to the experiences they had accumulated up to that point in time. Not that either generation—new school or old school—is necessarily better in any way, because every generation from every city has both busters *and* static-addicts, but, I say it because gangs have evolved, and the Hoovers are no exception. The time period in which the Hoover transplants arrived, helps determine which version of the gang the clone has been introduced to.

This is why it is so important in knowing your history, to include the quality and character of the original transplants, and the era in which they arrived.

For example, the Hoovers were Crips when they arrived in Portland. It wasn't until circa 1997 that the majority of the Hoovers dropped the use of the term Crip and assumed the use of the term Criminal in identifying ourselves. Even then, it wasn't something that we did independently. It was only embraced after years of

rumors circulating and originating from sources that did

not include any of the Hoover transplants who'd

originally cloned us.

The caliber of the clones in the beginning was a

reflection of the collection of individual Hoovers who

arrived. (at least one was a stone-cold serial killer—(HIP

Herm). Introductions were only possible to begin with

because of the like-minded-ness shared between the

original meetings of minds that met when the L.A.

transplants arrived.

Similarly, there are other L.A. gangs in Portland

that have clones created by transplants who were instead

busters and those original clones ended up being like-

minded busters that spawned generation after generation

of future busters.

A similar discussion could be had about the adaptability of the transplants from L.A. and the differences they are confronted with when they got somewhere new. Many were the hustler type and it was that which drew them to where they pulled up at. Some had or developed drug addictions that would fade them away from gang activity. Others were facing third strikes and simply looking for a potential extension of freedom.

Some would die in gun battles, and other transplants would get life sentences for *putting in work* in such hardcore criminal episodes that they'd come to define the way that law enforcement, courts, prisons, and news outlets all over America regarded gangs from L.A. as particularly troublesome.

You couldn't discuss interaction between Hoovers from L.A. and those from elsewhere, without talking about originality and even more important than that, how it spread. In most instances, it was the L.A.

Hoovers who went to a town, put their flag in the ground, and recruited new members in that city. There are other instances , however, where Homies moved to L.A. from elsewhere and got put on the set in L.A. before moving on and then spreading it out elsewhere themselves.

This was what happened when some Belizeans, who moved to L.A. and became Crips, got deported to Belize where they took their Cripping back with 'em. To this day, if you go to Belize you'll see lots of Crips (and Bloods).

Because Hoover was spread more by L.A. Hoovers spreading it across the map, it almost has an undeniable natural sequence of an L.A. Hoover transplant outranking any clones by seniority alone. I think this remains unsaid, but simply calculated and understood by most.

What I've seen in the past is that there are two
main types attitudes held by *L.A.* Hoovers towards *out-of-town* Hoovers. The first type is of a respectful nature,
a man respecting another man—proud to meet someone
who admires their own gang, indeed, so much that they
joined it, *represent* it, and helps to hold the flag down
despite never having been to the specific neighborhood
the gang was based on and in. This is the type of L.A.
Hoover who will respect loyalty and exchange his own
in a common practice of the universal principles for
which they stand together for. He will do so because he
recognizes and respects that the principles are what the
gang is centered on and not the turf alone.

The other type of attitude I've experienced is
that of a disrespectful nature—an L.A. gang member
who arrives in a city other than his own and behaves
arrogantly and ignorantly, superior (in their own minds)
of any of the local clones. This type of L.A. "Homie"

sees the local clones as expendable because in their mind,
a clone is not *really* from their gang.

L.A. Hoovers should, but don't always, know
that when they meet an out-of-town Hoover for the first
time, these are some of the things that are being weighed
in their out-of-town yet *in-town* frame of mind, meaning
that when an L.A Hoover is perceived as the former and
not the latter of the types described above, the thought
becomes, "this is *my* city."

My own personal anecdote is seeing all men as
men or as being mice. I extend unto other men the
respect which is due to them, and I'll smush a mouse and
throw 'em out my house. Really though, I believe that
most men, L.A. Hoovers, or any other gang members,
would do the same thing. The truth of the matter is really
in the answer to the greater question of: *are you man or
mouse?*

The Truth about White Members of Black Gangs

by Upton O'Goode

In most contexts, with the polar extremities of views being out there, discussing race can almost always be become controversial, especially if you're white and you make an attempt to define the *black experience. But,* if you're black in a black gang and you're discussing a white member, then, by all means, you white boys better listen up!

First of all, you white boys are **outsiders** no matter how long you've been around black people. No matter how black your speech accent is or how many black women you have babies by, you are white and will never be black.

You joined a gang and the gang did not join you. In that order, do not forget that loyalty for us, more so when pertaining to *you*, is to that of the gang and not to you or your white race. If you want to get by as a member of our gang, you also better understand that it is predominantly a black gang, so adapt accordingly *white boy*.

Another adjustment that is mandatory you grow accustomed to is the fact that you'll *never* be a **man** in the eyes of your comrades; it's why they'll refer to you as a (white) *boy*, even if you live long enough to become old. Last, but not least on that note, don't you ever in your life refer to one of your black comrades as a boy or we'll beat your ass!

Also, don't go thinking that each and every one of you will be accepted into a black gang. We only allow a few at a time, mostly as mascots, because you gotta admit that it's cute when you see a white boy throwing up the set and talking like he's black. It's our revenge for the Uncle Toms and house slaves who sell out their own people for the white folks—you know:*your* people.

We *do* see in you white boys a certain performance that indicates advanced loyalty, but because we can't understand *why* you'd be as loyal as you seem to be to us, we'll never be as loyal to you as you *probably* are to us.

We see you as softer than us. That doesn't say that you're soft per se, however, we just look at ourselves in our black skin as being tougher in every regard. Pound for pound, we'll likely win in a fight just as we would a basketball game; and, of course, our dicks are bigger than yours so the women, especially your white women, are gonna prefer us over you on a regular and frequent basis. Don't panic though, we'll leave you some—*you the Homie!*

Remember not to overextend yourself towards

excellence either. If you begin appearing as though you

are doing better than any of us, we'll certainly regard

you with disdain and we'll politick on you so fast, that

you won't know *what* happened.

Your best bet as a white boy is to be as quiet as

you can and just go with the flow of whatever your

Homies are doing at any given time. Your role as a white

boy is merely a supporting role, meaning you will never

be a turf-all-star or shot-caller, so don't you ever try to

be because you will only find out how weak you really

are in the shadows of real black men who will out-do

you in every aspect of the world we live in.

Your views, ideals, and opinions, no matter how

sound and reasonable they may be, are unimportant to us.

You can keep that bullshit, because the fact that it came

from you and not one of us is evidence in itself that it's

not strong enough for us to subscribe to. Get in the

backseat white boy, or else get away from the car!

If you white boys think that any or all of this is

unfair, no one is forcing you to join. You can always go

join an outlaw motorcycle gang, the skinheads, or the Ku

Klux Klan. Since they don't accept black members, you

wouldn't have to deal with any of the discrimination

discussed herein.

Frankly, you're disgusting and we really can't

stand you. We amuse ourselves by having you around

for as long as you'll endure the abuse we have set out for

you, and when you're gone, we'll openly talk about how

much we couldn't stand "that whiteboy."

It's no big deal for us whether you join, leave, or

if you stick around and take it—the way we see it is that

you were never truly one of us because you never could

be. We just played along with it to entertain ourselves

with your desperation to be like us. It's like the old
saying goes: *imitation is the sincerest form of flattery.*
Well, we're flattered, but it still doesn't make you one of
us.

If you're a white boy, keep these things in mind
before committing to us. We don't want to hear all sorts
of excuses or complaints; just submit your loyalty and
make the sacrifices expected of you.

If you see some us subscribing to hypocrisy, or
otherwise condoning behavior and actions of black
members that are inconsistent with certain principles and
ideals for which we have verbally made clear that we do
or don't live by, such as snitching or running from a
fight, and you see that there are little to no consequences
for those actions/inactions, do not confuse yourself by
thinking you can do these things and that they'll
similarly be ignored or downplayed.

If **YOU**, a white boy, do *anything* outside of what is considered righteous, *you're outta here!* There will be no resumption of normal activities. There will be no forgiveness or second chances. There'll be no discipline for you either; you will become excluded and exiled and talked about like the buster you are—simply because we never saw you as anything more than that to begin with. Get it?

Shout out to all the white Homies! Throw it up, throw it up, throw it up!

The Truth about Survival

by Reverend Robby Ray

The truth about survival is that it takes much of

the same frame of mind in most situations in which there

is such a necessity calling for it. I won't soak you in

what I mean. Instead, I'll share with you some shit the

Army has shared with all of us, yet many people, for

some reason, just don't read the shit (truth!).

The following is an excerpt from the Army Field

Manual for Survival, consciously apply it into your own

perspective of the streets or prison:

The following paragraphs expand on the meaning of each letter of the word SURVIVAL. Study and remember what each letter signifies because some day you may have to make the word work for you.

S—SIZE UP THE SITUATION

If you are in a combat situation, find a place where you can conceal yourself from the enemy. Remember, security takes priority. Use your senses of hearing, smell, and sight to get a feel for the battle-space. Determine if the enemy is attacking, defending, or withdrawing. You will have to consider what is developing on the battle-space when you make your survival plan.

Surroundings

Determine the pattern of the area. Get a feel for what is going on around you. Every environment, whether forest, jungle, or desert, has a rhythm or pattern; this tempo includes animal and bird noises and movements and insect sounds. It may also include enemy traffic and civilian movements.

Physical Condition

The pressure of the battle you were in or the trauma of being in a survival situation may have caused you to overlook wounds you received. Check your wounds and give yourself first aid. Take care to prevent further bodily harm. For instance, in any climate, drink plenty of water to prevent dehydration. If you are in a cold or wet climate, put on additional clothing to prevent hypothermia.

Equipment

Perhaps in the heat of battle, you lost or damaged some of your equipment. Check to see what equipment you have and what condition it is in.

Now that you have sized up your situation, surroundings, physical condition, and equipment, you are ready to make your survival plan. In doing so, keep in mind your basic physical needs—water, food, and shelter.

U—USE ALL YOUR SENSES, UNDUE HASTE MAKES WASTE

You may make a wrong move when you react quickly without thinking or planning. That move may result in your capture or death. Don't move just for the sake of taking action. Consider all aspects of your situation before you make a decision and a move. If you act in haste, you may forget or lose some of your equipment. In your haste you may also become disoriented so that you don't know which way to go. Plan your moves. Be ready to move out quickly without endangering yourself if the enemy is near you. Use all your senses to evaluate the situation. Note sounds and smells. Be sensitive to temperature changes. Always be observant.

R—REMEMBER WHERE YOU ARE

Spot your location on your map and relate it to the surrounding terrain. This basic principle is one that you must always follow. If there are other persons with you, make sure they also know their location. Always know who in your group, vehicle, or aircraft has a map and compass. If that person is killed, you will have to get the map and compass from him. Pay close attention to where you are and where you are going. Do not rely on others in the group to keep track of the route. Constantly orient yourself. Always try to determine, as a minimum, how your location relates to the location of—

• Enemy units and controlled areas.

• Friendly units and controlled areas.

• Local water sources (especially important in the desert).

• Areas that will provide good cover and concealment.

This information will allow you to make intelligent decisions when you are in a survival and evasion situation.

V—VANQUISH FEAR AND PANIC

The greatest enemies in a combat survival and evasion situation are fear and panic. If uncontrolled, they can destroy your ability to make an intelligent decision. They may cause you to react to your feelings and imagination rather than to your situation. These emotions can drain your energy and thereby cause other negative emotions. Previous survival and evasion training and self-confidence will enable you to vanquish fear and panic.

<u>I—IMPROVISE</u>

In the United States (U.S.), we have items available for all our needs. Many of these items are cheap to replace when damaged. Our easy-come, easy-go, easy-to-replace culture makes it unnecessary for us to improvise. This inexperience in "making do" can be an enemy in a survival situation. Learn to improvise.

Take a tool designed for a specific purpose and see how many other uses you can make of it.

Learn to use natural objects around you for different needs.

An example is using a rock for a hammer. No matter how complete a survival kit you have with you, it will run out or wear out after a while. Your imagination must take over when your kit wears out.

<u>V—VALUE LIVING</u>

191

All of us were born kicking and fighting to live, but we have become used to the soft life. We have become creatures of comfort.

We dislike inconveniences and discomforts. What happens when we are faced with a survival situation with its stresses, inconveniences, and discomforts? This is when the will to live—placing a high value on living—is vital. The experience and knowledge you have gained through life and your Army training will have a bearing on your will to live. Stubbornness, a refusal to give in to problems and obstacles that face you, will give you the mental and physical strength to endure.

A—ACT LIKE THE NATIVES

The natives and animals of a region have adapted to their environment. To get a feel of the area, watch how the people go about their daily routine. When and what do they eat? When, where, and how do they get their food? When and where do they go for water? What time do they usually go to bed and get up?

These actions are important to you when you are trying to avoid capture.

Animal life in the area can also give you clues on how to survive. Animals also require food, water, and shelter. By watching them, you can find sources of water and food.

Keep in mind that the reaction of animals can reveal your presence to the enemy.

If in a friendly area, one way you can gain rapport with the natives is to show interest in their tools and how they get food and water. By studying the people, you learn to respect them, you often make valuable friends, and, most important, you learn how to adapt to their environment and increase your chances of survival.

L—LIVE BY YOUR WITS, BUT FOR NOW, LEARN BASIC SKILLS

Without training in basic skills for surviving and evading on the battle-space, your chances of living through a combat survival and evasion situation are slight.

Learn these basic skills now—not when you are headed for or are in the battle. How you decide to equip yourself before deployment will affect whether or not you survive. You need to know about the environment to which you are going, and you must practice basic skills geared to that environment. For instance, if you are going to a desert, you need to know how to get water.

The entire Army Field Manual for Survival is a publication in the public domain and can be found free on many online websites simply by searching for it by name. I, personally recommend it as some of the most helpful knowledge you could ever acquire living in this world we live in. Survival isn't always about surviving the streets. The streets are just one of many habitats in which the same skills could apply and could come in handy one day. The truth about survival is that if you can't do it, you'll die.

Afterword

by Tyrone Suess

I want to conclude this book by thanking everyone who took the time to read it. If you've read it and have sudden desire to throw it in the trash, thanks for buying it.

If you hated it more than that and would rather kill us, get in line with everyone else. It's been the story of this life. Anything we live for should be worth dying for. I live to write so it's just gonna have to be whatever it is with me.

All negativity to the side, I truly appreciate every one of you who have supported this endeavor. I'll leave you with a reminder that the truth is purely and philosophically what you perceive it to be, so there was no harm intended if you've been hurt by anything written. Perhaps these truths will stimulate further discussion that will ultimately preserve a more in-depth history altogether; in that way, we all win.